MW01075584

HOLY GROUND

HOLY GROUND

ON ACTIVISM, ENVIRONMENTAL JUSTICE, *and* FINDING HOPE

Catherine Coleman Flowers

Spiegel and Grau

S&G

Spiegel & Grau, New York
www.spiegelandgrau.com

Interior design by Meighan Cavanaugh

Library of Congress Cataloging-in-Publication Data Available Upon Request

ISBN (hardcover) 978-1-954118-68-3
ISBN (eBook) 978-1-954118-69-0

Printed in the United States on 30% postconsumer recycled paper

First Edition
10 9 8 7 6 5 4 3 2 1

For K. J., Halo, and
seven generations to come.

If I speak in the tongues of men or of angels, but do not have love, I am only a resounding gong or a clanging cymbal. If I have the gift of prophecy and can fathom all mysteries and all knowledge, and if I have a faith that can move mountains, but do not have love, I am nothing...

Love is patient, love is kind. It does not envy, it does not boast, it is not proud. It does not dishonor others, it is not self-seeking, it is not easily angered, it keeps no record of wrongs. Love does not delight in evil but rejoices with the truth. It always protects, always trusts, always hopes, always perseveres.

—1 Corinthians 13:1–2, 4–7

CONTENTS

HOLY GROUND

Prologue

I HAVE LIVED MANY LIVES, A GREAT BLESSING.

I have been in the military and on the red carpet. I have been a high school teacher in marginalized and underfunded schools and an environmental justice activist who has sat among world leaders. I am the recipient of a MacArthur "Genius" grant and have been the victim of terrifying sexual abuse. I have sat with poor families in their substandard homes and I have escorted members of Congress, presidential advisers, and officials from the Department of Justice to visit with them as well.

I am the oldest of five children, proudly hailing from Lowndes County, Alabama. I am the mother of an amazing daughter and the grandmother of two.

I am the recipient of an honorary doctorate from a prestigious university. I am a historian.

I have sat at the feet of great and noble teachers: preachers of the social gospel, respected academics, and visionary leaders of historic change.

I am a Christian and a woman who knows that the only reason I am where I am is because of God's grace and mercy.

I am the author of a memoir that chronicles my evolution as an environmental justice activist and my work on behalf of poor and rural families.

I have written this collection of essays in order to reflect on this moment we are living through. These essays have provided an opportunity for me to contextualize the present with perspective from the past, from the Revolutionary War to the Cold War, from Reconstruction to the halls of Congress in the twenty-first century. My work has been fueled by lessons learned from history. I've also learned that perspective and faith can offer timeless resonance and comfort: perspective on the grand struggles and historic events that have brought us to this point; faith that we can make it through.

In telling these stories, I have learned new narratives about myself.

I am reminded of a wonderful short poem, "Final Curve," by the great poet Langston Hughes:

> When you turn the corner
> And you run into yourself
> Then you know that you have turned
> All the corners that are left

I have not yet turned all the corners in my life. But in turning corners from the past, I have run into myself. I have come to realize that my story and the stories of others who have turned corners of their own may hold lessons we can all learn from.

That is my hope and my prayer as you join me.

Huntsville, Alabama,
June 2024

ONE

Thirty Pieces of Silver

Judas Iscariot is a complicated figure in the New Testament. Once one of Jesus's favorite disciples, Judas betrayed Christ for thirty pieces of silver. And his final gesture was a kiss— a cynical way to end a close friendship. "Whomever I kiss, He is the one; seize him," Judas said to the Roman authorities. He had made a deal with the Romans to hand over Jesus in exchange for payment and was intoxicated with his power. I can see him before his deception, imagining how he would spend the money he would receive. "Greetings, Rabbi," Judas said, and he kissed Jesus. "But Jesus asked him, 'Judas, are you betraying the Son of Man with a kiss?'" (Luke 22:48), a reproachful question, a resigned rebuke.

After witnessing the torture and death of his Lord, Judas was so consumed by guilt and regret that he hung himself. His story has come to embody a timeless fable of greed at the expense of human decency. "Judas" has become shorthand for treachery and the human inclination to sell our souls for a relatively meaningless sum in an attempt to grasp power, or revenge, or wealth. Judas was an essential actor in fulfilling the purpose of Jesus on Earth— only through his betrayal would Jesus suffer and die for our sins, and then rise again from the dead. But as Matthew writes in 26:24, "The Son of man will go just as it is written about him. But woe to that man who betrays the Son of man! It would be better for him if he had not been born."

It would be better for him if he had not been born.

I have thought of Judas often over the years. Sometimes with compassion for the remorse he quickly felt, the anguish he must have experienced as he fulfilled his destiny on Earth. I have also thought of him with contempt. Back in Jesus's time, thirty pieces of silver were worth about four months' wages—a nice cushion but hardly life-changing. For so little money, a former intimate stabbed his friend and mentor in the back. He deprived his community of a consummate healer and teacher. And he earned a place in infamy.

Today, I see how versions of those thirty pieces of silver are responsible for evil in so many places, affecting people of all incomes, all races, all social and geographical realms. In the horrifying and senseless deaths of children from gun violence. In the abandonment of causes by people who used to be advocates. In the destruction of the hard-won right to vote through gerrymandering and bogus legal challenges. In the hypocrisy of religious leaders whose lives contradict the values they teach. Those pieces of silver have become a compelling metaphor for many of the harms inflicted on innocent people because of the enormous profits a very few enjoy—whether they are politicians, corporate giants, or the random billionaire determined to inflict his will on others by purchasing the time and influence of those in power. And I despair as I watch once-trusted elected officials, once-revered members of the judiciary, or once-respected religious leaders wrap themselves in rectitude as they sell out people who are less fortunate.

We used to talk about "dark money," about the enormous amount of funds funneled through various channels that slip through disclosure requirements. This money is designed to influence politicians, to put a thumb on the scale in favor of wealth and influence—both political parties are guilty of it. The nonpartisan Brennan Center notes that more than a billion dollars have been spent influencing federal elections since the 2010 *Citizens United* case, in which the Supreme Court ruled that money in politics is basically an expression of free speech and therefore should not be constrained. If this is all about free speech, which one might see as transparent, then why is secrecy so important? If the cause is righteous enough to support, why not consider the donation an example to be replicated? One reason that secrecy, that darkness became important is that it made it impossible for voters to know who is doing the influencing and why. Without transparency, truly informed decisions when choosing members of Congress, state judges, governors, mayors, or the president of the United States become impossible.

And yet, as I look around, I am struck by how much of this dirty dealing is taking place in broad daylight. Billionaires, corporations, and some of our political and religious leaders are doing what Judas did more than two thousand years ago—minus any shame or remorse. Today, it seems as if undermining our democratic system—which may not be perfect, but it's one of the best ideas ever to have appeared—is worthy of large investment. At end of the day, these interests don't want democracy at all. They want control. And if you bring the cause of this crisis back to a single common denominator, it is thirty pieces of silver.

IN 1999, WHEN I WORKED in a Detroit high school teaching social studies and government classes, I had the pleasure of working with a very talented group of students in the public school system. These were the kids who would consume every bit of knowledge that was put in front of them, hungry to perform for a teacher not just for a grade but to expand their minds and widen their vision of the world and their potential role in it. I always loved being a teacher. I loved seeing how children grew as they learned, almost as if you could measure it with a mark on the kitchen wall—except these growth spurts were all internal. Teaching and learning, when it was all in sync, became an intellectual and also almost a visual experience for me. I could see something in my students' eyes, something in the way they walked, or talked, that showed a new and positive self-confidence.

Even for the students who may not have been academically gifted, school was a special place—and maybe the only secure space in their lives. This was where they would be guaranteed two meals a day, Monday through Friday. For many children who came from disjointed, troubled families, school became the one refuge in their lives. A place where all the chaos around them melted into a predictable and reassuring routine. As long as there have been schools, I imagine there have always been troublemakers and bullies and unhappy kids determined to share their unhappiness with others. But even with all that, even with some children facing difficult dynamics, the fundamental safety a child experienced when they walked through the school doors could be depended on.

Until, that is, April 20, 1999, when Eric Harris and Dylan Klebold strode into Columbine High School in Jefferson County, Colorado, with an arsenal of weapons—from explosives to semi-automatic rifles—in their duffel bags. Columbine is a small community south of Denver of about twenty thousand people, 85 percent of them white. Harris and Klebold were in their senior year. They initially put bombs in the cafeteria at lunchtime, but the bombs failed to detonate. So the boys took their positions and began to shoot students randomly. The first victim was a girl who was innocently eating lunch with a friend at the school's entrance. In only thirty minutes, as terror swept through the school, they murdered twelve students and one teacher and injured more than twenty-one others, until, finally, they turned the guns on themselves.

And just like that, school was not a safe place anymore. The threats began in my school in Detroit soon afterward. One day, someone had written on a wall that on a particular day there would be a shooting in the school. The principal called the teachers into her office and told us that if we didn't feel comfortable, we didn't need to come to school that day. I told my father, and he asked me to stay at home. So did my daughter, Taylor, who was just a small child at the time. But I felt I needed to go in. Wearing jeans and running shoes, I went to school. I had an escape route planned, through the window into the street. They had asked us to gather in the auditorium, which I thought was ill-advised. And at one point during the day, police came to sweep the school. Fortunately, the threat proved false. Clearly, though, nothing would be the same again.

There have been more than two thousand school shootings since Columbine, and since 2015, for some reason, the numbers have skyrocketed. In 2023 alone, there were nearly 350 school shootings across the country. In looking at data from 1966 to 2024, a total of 2,239 victims were wounded and 816 victims were killed in K–12 shootings. Of those, 20.9 percent took place in elementary schools, 10.9 percent were in middle schools, and an astonishing 61.4 percent occurred in high schools. Despite the frequency, some still have the power to shock and remain prominent in the national memory: the twenty tiny elementary school children and six adults massacred at Sandy Hook Elementary School in Newtown, Connecticut, in 2012; the Valentine's Day shooting at Marjory Stoneman Douglas High School in Parkland, Florida, in 2018, when a nineteen-year-old with an AR-15 murdered seventeen students and injured seventeen others; and then again at Santa Fe High School, in Santa Fe, Texas, only a few months later, when a seventeen-year-old student used his father's .38 revolver and shotgun to kill eight students and two teachers and injure thirteen more.

Then there was the shooting in Uvalde, Texas, a town of about fifteen thousand people, nearly 80 percent of whom are Hispanic. The town is located in the southernmost point of the Texas Hill Country, about an hour from the Mexican border. The mass shooting at Robb Elementary School took place on May 24, 2022. The toll: nineteen children and two teachers were killed and seventeen others were injured. The delayed police response—they waited one hour and fourteen minutes before storming the building—is one of the reasons why the death toll was so high. That, and the AR-15 military-style rifle the shooter used.

School was not the only place where safety seemed to be a given that was shattered by gun violence; churches were too. When I was growing up, if my music was turned up when I passed by a church, I would turn it down just as a respectful reflex. Now we see guns in many places where they should never be, creating tragedies that dominate the national conversation until the next one. Twenty-six people were killed in a mass shooting at First Baptist Church of Sutherland Springs, Texas, in 2017. That was two years after Dylann Roof walked into the Emanuel African Methodist Episcopal Church in Charleston, South Carolina, and shot nine Black people quietly engaged in Bible study that evening in 2015. I have attended similar Bible-study sessions. I could have been one of them, or my parents, or my siblings, or my friends could have been. Eleven lives were lost in 2018 at the Tree of Life Synagogue shooting in Pittsburgh, Pennsylvania.

I cannot calculate the enormity of these tragedies on the communities whose grief and anxiety will never go away. What have we lost in talent and treasure because of the oft-repeated refusal of our government to enact anything resembling meaningful gun laws? How many "thoughts and prayers" or "this is not a gun issue, it is a mental health issue" bromides must substitute for action that would make a difference? My father believed in responsible gun ownership. He owned guns and taught us never, ever to lay a hand on them. And naturally, we obeyed him. We lived in rural communities where people learned how to shoot. My brothers were expert marksmen, my sister too. But they all knew what it meant to be a responsible gun owner.

Nowadays, is there any more explicit example of our thirty pieces of silver than the way the National Rifle Association has so thoroughly compromised lawmakers in nearly every state in the union? No matter how innocent the victims, how massive the tragedy, how pervasive the effect throughout our society, or how many people want controls on assault weapons? Compared with Germany, the United States has seventy-seven times the rate of homicides with guns; compared with France, we have 17 percent more gun-related deaths; and compared with Australia, we have thirty-three times the rate of gun-related deaths.

Texas has an unusually high number of these incidents—including Uvalde, the church in Sutherland Springs, and of course the 2019 massacre at the El Paso Walmart. At least twenty mass shootings have killed more than two hundred people in the state over the past sixty years, according to the *Texas Tribune*. And that does not begin to factor in the individual lives lost from smaller incidents in the home, or during a robbery, or when someone makes a mistake or dies by suicide. Hands are wrung, tears are shed, but in Texas, for the past six decades, every single measure to control guns has been defeated. Any one of them could have changed the outcome of these tragedies. The year of the Uvalde massacre, the NRA poured more than $5 million into the coffers of Texas elected officials to ensure that, in effect, it was just a matter of time before another Uvalde would happen again.

I am sure that nearly everyone who refuses to vote for sensible gun control congratulates themselves on being good Bible-reading Christians, confident that "the good guy with the gun" will be present to defeat the forces of evil. I am surprised that they have missed the many passages that focus on the love and care that Jesus had for children. "I have no greater joy than to hear that my children are walking in the truth," John 1:4 tells us. Matthew especially focuses on tender words for children. "See that you do not despise one of these little ones. For I tell you that their angels in heaven always see the face of my Father in heaven," he writes in 18:10. Only a few verses earlier, Jesus says, "If anyone causes one of these little ones—those who believe in me—to stumble, it would be better for them to have a large millstone hung around their neck and to be drowned in the depths of the sea."

"Drowned in the depths of the sea" is the consequence if anyone merely causes an innocent to stumble. I wonder what Jesus would say today.

In Lowndes County, Alabama, we went to church every Sunday, often not for a formal service but always for Sunday school. My parents were both devout Christians, my mother a member of the Missionary Baptist Church, which, like the name suggests, was committed to missionary work as a way to spread the Word of God to those who had not received it. They began in the early nineteenth century, a splinter group of the Baptists who were generally not inclined to venture out and proselytize. Theirs was part of an important story that began in 1886, when the National Baptist Convention was organized by a group of Black believers to diminish the influence of white national bodies. The movement took hold, so by 1895, three million Black Baptists, mostly in the South, called themselves members of the National Baptist

Convention of America. Today, they are a part of the National Baptist Association. My mother attended the Missionary Baptist church in her home county of Autauga.

My father, however, was a member of another historically Black church, the Christian Methodist Episcopal (CME). Created after the Civil War by forty-one formerly enslaved members of the Methodist Episcopal Church in Jackson, Tennessee, they too splintered off to create their own religious organization. Today it is a 1.5 million–member multiracial and international denomination in the US, Haiti, Jamaica, and nations in Africa. One of Alabama's notable Historically Black Colleges and Universities (HBCUs), Miles College in Birmingham, is CME affiliated.

For as long as I can remember, elders would teach us from a well-worn book of lessons from the Old and the New Testament, and still today, many of those lessons resonate powerfully with me. I loved the story of Jonah, for instance, who was saved from drowning by being washed into the belly of a whale—who thoughtfully "vomited Jonah out upon dry land" after three days so the prophet would be able to return to Nineveh and teach the word of God that his early cowardice had prevented.

Then there were the three brave men with the lyrical names that children delighted in saying: Shadrach, Meshach, and Abednego. They refused to bow to the golden image King Nebuchadnezzar (another fine name!) had erected, believing that God would save them from any punishment—if not in this world, then the next. The king was outraged by their disobedience, even as all "the satraps, prefects, governors, advisers, treasurers, judges, magistrates and all the other provincial officials" (Daniel 3–6) did what they had been told. The three apostates were thrown into a fiery furnace by the enraged king but, miraculously, were invulnerable to the flames: "The fire had not harmed their bodies, nor was a hair of their heads singed; their robes were not scorched, and there was no smell of fire on them" (Daniel 3:27). But the three men were not alone in the flames: the Son of man had joined them. Nebuchadnezzar's rage crumbled in the face of this miracle and was replaced by faith, and for the rest of his forty-three-year reign he became known as "God's servant."

I think of the burning bush revealing God's voice to Moses. Moses was a simple man, tending sheep, when he saw a bush ablaze but not consumed by fire. As he approaches this unusual phenomenon, God speaks to him and anoints him as the leader of his chosen people—a seemingly overwhelming job but one that, despite all the odds against him, he undertook for forty years. He moved the people of Israel from slavery to freedom, coping with their doubt and complaints and the dangers the journey involved. He witnessed how tempted they were by various versions of those pieces of silver and spent so much of his time trying to persuade them this was not the path they should take. And yet, in what seems a painful injustice, Moses never reached the Promised Land.

Satan tempted Jesus too, three times during the forty days Jesus spent in the wilderness fasting and praying. Satan offered to turn stones into bread, he urged Jesus to throw himself from the temple, and he offered him vast earthly power for the simple act of submission. All of which, of course, Jesus refused.

There are so many other stories, but the ones that have always held special meaning for me are those that focused on overcoming adversity and staying faithful—precisely the opposite of what Judas did. These lessons are timeless and hold as true today as they have for millennia. Adversity does not just mean being enslaved by the Egyptians or betrayed by Judas. And overcoming adversity is not arriving at the Promised Land or Jesus having risen from the dead to redeem us all. Today our mission is to defeat the systems that perpetuate racism, injustice, poverty, and the deep divisions among us, as toxic as the smoke spewing from factories or the waste from deteriorating septic systems. Many of the indelible lessons from the Bible are about the triumph over earthly temptation. One of the lessons we can take from the thirty pieces of silver is that the simple choices we make can have dire consequences.

ONE OF THOSE OSTENSIBLY SIMPLE CHOICES takes place every four years when we cast our ballots in order to answer a profoundly important question: Who would be the best person to lead our country? When more people vote for one person instead of another, they provide the answer—for the next four years. Representative democracy is a simple and straightforward process. And yet, how riddled with injustice it has been throughout history. After all, when the vote was initially extended in this country, it was only for white male property owners. Then, after the Civil War, during Reconstruction, Black men briefly had the right to vote, but nearly insurmountable barriers stood in their paths. And it was only in 1919 that the suffragettes secured voting rights for women.

The expansion of the franchise to as many people as possible was the central component of the battle for civil rights, and that involved making it easier to register to vote. The ultimate goal was civil rights, not just for those who had been historically disenfranchised but for all Americans. Ending injustice that had existed within the electoral system would make that system more robust, more durable, more incorruptible. This is the essence of democracy. The 1965 Voting Rights Act was a long-overdue miracle, lowering the voting age from twenty-one to eighteen years old, eliminating literacy tests and poll taxes, and providing people with language barriers or disabilities new access to exercise their rights.

But the pernicious allure of money and power and, in some cases, revenge—Biblical narratives in their modern forms—have distorted what should be a straightforward democratic process. Sometimes these forces are at play with an individual politician, cheerfully accepting enormous campaign contributions in exchange for favorable votes or a piece of legislation. In other cases, those forces have infected a whole state, or an entire political party, or a justice system. Yes, in our democracy, voting can right the wrongs. Unless the process of voting once again is undermined.

Shelby County v. Holder, decided in 2013, is a case referred to as the Supreme Court decision that "gutted" the Voting Rights Act. Everything is just fine, Justice Roberts seemed to say when writing for the majority. In this time of racial equality, states don't need to have the Department of Justice looking over their shoulders to ensure free and fair elections. If one wanted evidence of why the chief justice was wrong, one needed only to look at the twenty-three states that imposed new restrictions on voting in the wake of this decision. Voter rolls were purged, voter ID requirements were instituted, polling places were closed or their hours restricted, and highly partisan administrators started monitoring elections with the single-minded objective of making voting harder rather than easier.

Partisan gerrymandering experienced a vibrant renaissance. All over the country, new voting districts were redrawn to advantage one party—usually the GOP, but not always—over the other. The process is pretty straightforward when one party dominates a state legislature: first, redraw the maps to benefit your party, then send the new maps to the state legislature for approval, and finally get ready to have even more power come the next election. Often, but not always, the gerrymandering has a racist cast to it by diluting the power of Black voters.

This is what had happened in Alabama, but in 2022, three judges in a federal court concluded that my state had violated the Voting Rights Act by not creating another Black-majority congressional district. In fact, the proposed district went straight through the Black Belt, and the amicus brief from Alabama historians noted several distinguishing factors: "The Black Belt is a community of interest joined by socioeconomic, political, and geographical factors." Its population "shares a historic identity: slaves concentrated amidst extreme planter class wealth." In addition, "The Black Belt population experiences intense economic hardship." Moreover, "Black Belt residents lack—and have lacked for more than a century—access to basic social services, including healthcare and education."

Even though the court made their decision very clearly, and the Supreme Court affirmed it, compelling Alabama to draw another majority-Black district, state Republicans decided to take matters into their own hands. They redrew the district so that only 40 percent of the voters were African American. Governor Kay Ivey was pleased that the state defied the courts. "The legislature knows our state, our people, and our districts better than the federal courts or activist groups," she said. In response, the federal court appointed a special master to redraw the maps in Alabama, resulting in one new majority-Black voting district. But all over the country in the lead-up to the 2024 elections, similar shenanigans were taking place: Florida's redistricting map was ruled as discriminating against Black voters, and there were challenges in Georgia and Louisiana. Wisconsin Republicans were way ahead of the game in disenfranchising urban areas that tended to vote Democratic.

The fight against voter suppression has been going on for quite some time. The civil rights leader Bishop William J. Barber II, co-chair of the Poor People's Campaign, is someone I consider a friend and an ally whose work is also driven by the social justice messages in the Gospels. In 2019, Barber (who was a reverend at that time) was convicted of second-degree trespassing at the North Carolina General Assembly during a protest against Republican efforts to gerrymander the voting map. State judges would describe the attempts to enact illegal voter-ID laws and undermine access to health care as having been executed with "surgical precision." When he went to the state legislature to meet with lawmakers, Reverend Barber was accompanied by a group that included doctors, mothers with cancer, preachers, and veterans. They chanted scripture. "Isaiah 10," he said. "Woe unto those who legislate evil and rob the poor of their rights." He then laid out the grim statistics about the denial of health care to 500,000 people—346,000 white, over 140,000 people of color, and 30,000 veterans. He also read the Constitution aloud. The lawmakers refused to give him an audience.

In court, Reverend Barber was questioned by the prosecuting attorney about his behavior at the North Carolina General Assembly. He accused Reverend Barber of being disruptive. The exchange goes to the heart of the kind of activism that has been an essential part of a long tradition, one that often seems in danger of disappearing.

ATTORNEY: Is it your testimony that you were not yelling in that video?

REV. WILLIAM BARBER II: I would never characterize call and response, preaching, reading the Constitution, reading scripture as "yelling." Yelling insinuates a whole other type of state of mind, that you are somehow angry or whatnot. I was in a situation where I was using the voice that I've been given, and I was reciting [a] call and response to the Constitution, passages of scripture, and statistics about people that are hurting in this state because of denial of health care.

ATTORNEY: But your voice is louder than it is right now, wasn't it?

REVEREND BARBER: My voice? I'm not reciting. Yes, I'm not reciting the Constitution. I'm not engaging—

ATTORNEY: On that day, it was louder than it is right now, correct?

REVEREND BARBER: Sure.

ATTORNEY: But it's your testimony that you were not yelling in that video.

REVEREND BARBER: I would not characterize [it as] yelling.

ATTORNEY: And that perhaps you can make your voice even louder than that.

REVEREND BARBER: I'm not—I don't know what—how you're characterizing. I'm a preacher. And in the African

American tradition of preaching, in the evangelical tradition of preaching, in the Pentecostal tradition of preaching, there are ebbs and flows in our voice. That's all I can share with you.

I read the transcript and imagine a similar kind of interrogation taking place, say, in 1950. A distinguished Black preacher is chastised for "yelling," his expression of the Word demeaned as a kind of transgression—or maybe just bad manners. Or worse still, in the time of Jim Crow, a preacher being "uppity." But now something very different is going on. Yes, there is disrespect. But in response, Reverend Barber is using this cross-examination not only to demonstrate his innocence; he is also quietly, persistently, emphatically educating the prosecuting attorney.

And to that I say amen.

Reverend Barber in the North Carolina legislature was not only advocating for Black people. He was advocating for justice for everyone. When I advocate for sanitation, I am not single-mindedly concentrating on sanitation for people in the Black Belt of Alabama. I am advocating for sanitation for every poor person who needs it, every resident of every single rural community in our country, indeed in the world.

On the other hand, *The Guardian* reported that more than two dozen civil rights leaders in the South had been paid by regional power companies—who sometimes donated millions to organizations they ran—and then became their advocates, diverting "attention from the environmental harms that spew from their fossil fuel plants." Here we see the terrible potency of those thirty pieces of silver today in robbing some advocates of their moral compass. In contrast, Rev. Nelson Johnson, a Greensboro, North Carolina, pastor who'd encouraged the use of rooftop solar, believing that solar power helps all customers reduce their energy needs during a time of global warming, was visited three times by lobbyists paid by the state's Duke Energy company. In response, Reverend Johnson wrote a letter to the president and CEO of Duke Energy, calling out this "cynical and duplicitous corporate behavior." He wrote:

> It appears evident that this "solar hurts the poor" strategy has been coordinated by Duke and its cohorts in the corporate electric power industry and used in many states recently. Fortunately, the scheme has been rejected by the NAACP's national board, by various state NAACP chapters, and by the Congressional Black Caucus, among others. Nevertheless, Duke Energy is vigorously pursuing this same deception in North Carolina. This cynical corporate activity is an affront to the people of this state, and it is your personal responsibility to stop it. . . . Reducing the cost of electrical energy for the poor, while reducing North Carolina's carbon footprint through increased use of solar energy, reflects both moral and economic progress, which the broad religious community supports. We encourage Duke Energy to join us in this constructive undertaking. The other key element of your business plan is the persistent use of corporate influence to distort public debate and silence civic leaders, in an effort to protect Duke's profits from competition. All those elements seem to be active in this solar dispute. . . .

Increasingly, North Carolinians are coming together across traditional divisions. We will not be divided on this issue that is profoundly important for so many economic and environmental justice reasons. We call on Duke Energy to join those taking the lead toward a clean energy economy, not to remain in league with those who hold back the very positive changes that could spell the difference between a world of increasing cooperation and healthy communities, and one of devastating polarization.

Other power companies targeted Black community leaders to persuade them to stop discussing environmental problems caused by fossil fuel plants, and not everyone was as resolute as Reverend Johnson. In Alabama, one leader lobbied *against* the state when it attempted to lower electric bills. Rev. Michael Malcom, an old friend who watched this unfold, is the executive director of the Birmingham environmental justice organization Alabama Interfaith Power & Light. He explained his own version of thirty pieces of silver when he noted that a certain group of these so-called leaders "will sell you out because they'll sell anything—they'll sell seawater."

The Center for Earth Ethics and Kairos at the Union Theological Seminary, as well as the Poor People's Campaign, have shown that a critical and daunting aspect of the challenge we face to save the planet and save democracy is the transformation of our value system. Everywhere we turn, consumption and visions of wealth can easily upend priorities predicated on the common good. When we are barraged by overwhelming messages that celebrate the ephemeral, the self-involved, and transient pleasures, how is it possible to recalibrate our personal compasses? We worship together because it breaks the uncertainty that so often troubles us when we are alone. So too, acting together for social change—whether it is environmental justice or voting rights or economic fairness—reminds us that human solidarity can perform miracles. When I have marched, or worshipped, or demonstrated for climate justice, I am sustained by those who surround me.

When I was growing up, one of the African American spirituals we sang most regularly at church was "Go Down, Moses," a song popularized by the great actor and singer Paul Robeson and that was an anthem for enslaved people. It first appeared in sheet music back in 1853, written by a Rev. L. C. Lockwood, who was a chaplain ministering to fugitive slaves in Virginia.

When Israel was in Egypt's land
Let my people go
Oppress'd so hard they could not stand
Let my people go

Refrain:
Go down, Moses
Way down in Egypt's land
Tell old Pharaoh
Let my people go

The verse was from Exodus 9:1 in the Hebrew Bible: "This is what the Lord, the God of the Hebrews, says: 'Let my people go, so that they may worship me.'" This was when the struggle of the Jews for freedom from slavery began in earnest and unfolded in a series of challenges. But for enslaved Black people, the message was deeply personal. Someday, our ancestors would also escape the bounds of slavery; they would be "let go" and emerge, free.

That is the message that has been passed down about this important spiritual, but there is another layer of meaning that is often lost. The refrain of "Let my people go" appears several times in Exodus, but each time it does, it is not framed as a simple demand to Pharaoh for freedom; it is a clause preceding action. In the first instance, the Lord urges Moses to tell Pharaoh that the Hebrew people should have freedom "that they may *worship me*" (italics mine). Earlier in the story, the Lord instructs Moses to say to Pharaoh, "The Lord, the God of the Hebrews sent me to you to say, 'Let my people go, so that they *may worship me in the wilderness.*'" (Again, the italics are mine.) Let my people go so that they may *do* something with their freedom. Their freedom will be the opportunity for action. As a commentator on the Hebrew Bible wrote, "It was not only freedom *from* something; it was freedom *for* something."

And that, I think, is the answer to the question of how to transform values and replace the cynical allure of thirty pieces of silver with far more enduring and consequential compensation. The answer lies in action, in the movement *toward* a good that is shared by more than just a few. The soul-deep conviction that freedom *from* something must become freedom *for* something. And in that "something" resides vast fortunes—just not the kind that are easy to count and spend.

TWO

The Great Rural Divide

RURAL POVERTY IS INVISIBLE TO MOST URBAN DWELLERS. The rural poor may live in neglected rental properties. A family might be so worried about eviction or a rent hike that they don't want to call attention to the fact that the oven doesn't work and the toilet overflows because it's connected to a failing septic tank. Or maybe they live in a mobile home that started losing its value the moment it was towed off the lot. The roof and the floors are buckling from water damage. Temperature control doesn't exist, so the winters are unbearable for the cold—people are sick *all* the time—and the summers are unbearable for the heat. And they still owe $15,000 on the damn thing.

The rural poor live with their parents, maybe even their grandparents, and their kids. There never is enough money to cover food and clothes, utility payments, and anything that goes wrong—

and something always goes wrong. Checks from the government appear every month for the seniors, and sometimes the kids receive meager disability payments, and that's what keeps the family afloat. Thank God for food stamps. States like California and New York have raised their minimum wage to over fifteen dollars an hour, but for the rural poor in Alabama or Mississippi or South Carolina or Tennessee or Louisiana, which have no state minimum wage requirements, the federal minimum wage of $7.25 an hour still holds—the same rate since 2009. Even so, there aren't many jobs to be had in rural America, so working a minimum-wage job means driving to where one might be, and that means gas and car repairs. The money earned goes toward the care and feeding of a decades-old car with an internal combustion engine.

The rural poor live in agricultural communities, or maybe in towns that used to be almost prosperous from the local coal mines or factories that have been closed for years now. Or maybe they live a couple of miles off the interstate, not too far from a city but just far enough to qualify as rural, which is usually the word that precedes *poverty*. In these areas, everyone seems to be sick— with diabetes or heart disease or obesity or asthma. Childhood and maternal mortality rates are higher here than anywhere else in the country. By every measure the rural poor have worse health and educational outcomes. They are deprived of their fair share of the American dream. And over the years, the gap between the rural poor and the urban middle class has widened to the point of lunacy.

Poor rural kids attend the same schools their parents did. They were terrible then, and they're terrible now. Lockers are rusty, lunches look like fast food, school supplies are limited.

There are some devoted teachers who may see a spark in a child. They pay attention to these children as only gifted teachers can, and with the benefit of high-quality attention over a school year, a child may blossom. But how do you nourish that spark so it turns into the propulsion to get them the hell out and into a better life? If you can keep them safe and sound through middle school and high school, a period of six years in which every single day they are not in trouble—not tempted by opioids or meth or unsafe sex or something that will hurt or kill them—it feels like a blessing.

The rural poor are Black or brown or white or Indigenous, and if they share a common history, it is one of generations who haven't moved much beyond the confines of their communities. Education, the military, or sports offer a way out, a path for a few young people to improve their lot and maybe even offer some measure of relief for the rest of the family. Approximately forty-six million Americans live in rural communities in every state of the union, and more than seven million of them live in stubborn, relentless, abject poverty.

WHEN MOST PEOPLE THINK of rural communities, they assume the demographic is somehow exclusively white, but it's not. The history of rural communities is not just political and racial; it is cultural, and in that way poor Black people have a lot more in common with poor white people in these rural areas than they do with their urban counterparts. I am reminded of the criticism Beyoncé faced when she released a country music album—but I was country all my life. I know about Dolly Parton, Minnie Pearl,

Porter Wagoner, Earl Scruggs and Lester Flatt, and the Grand Ole Opry. I am the product of Black rural America.

I grew up poor in the 1960s, living with other poor people, in an Alabama community where people still used outhouses or, if we needed to relieve ourselves at night, "slop jars" that we emptied the next day. A back injury in his thirties forced my father to retire as a civil servant, but he ran a small business selling fish and watermelons off the back of his truck. My mother worked as a teacher's aid and drove the bus for students who had special needs. While we did without, we children were not deprived. We lived a country life, with hogs and a garden, so we never went hungry and ate the freshest food. The neighbors also had gardens, and we shared our produce. Fruit grew on trees, and berries were everywhere. We knew we were poor, but we all believed that there was a way out. A way out of poverty, a way to prosper someplace else. The intention, though, was to come back home and bring that good fortune back to the community. The difference now is, for many, there is no way out. Generational poverty is the norm rather than the exception.

In my work I have seen a lot of poverty. And I see a lot of inequality, especially in rural communities. When you put a sewage lagoon next to a Black community, those homes will lose their value. Consider the numbers: In urban areas, about 12 percent of residents live below the poverty line; in rural communities that number increases to 15.5 percent, with Mississippi, Louisiana, West Virginia, New Mexico, Arkansas, Kentucky, Oklahoma, Texas, New York, and, of course, Alabama featuring the highest poverty rates in the country. In those Southern states, the rural poverty rate is close to 20 percent, compared to the 13 percent

rate of rural poverty for those who live in the Midwest. A shocking 30 percent of rural Black people live in poverty, and, unsur-
prisingly, the South also is overrepresented in the statistics, with
Mississippi leading the way in the highest African American rural
poverty level in the nation at nearly 20 percent. According to the
US Department of Agriculture, which maintains these numbers,
poverty has been declining since it was first measured in 1960,
but that decline isn't evenly distributed throughout the country.
In my home state of Alabama, out of a total population of just
over five million, nearly 1.15 million individuals live in rural
communities—and of those rural residents, almost 20 percent
are poor. As the USDA states, "Concentrated poverty contributes
to poor housing and health conditions, higher crime and school
dropout rates, and employment dislocations. As a result, economic
conditions in very poor areas can create limited opportunities for
poor residents that become self-perpetuating." In other words,
poverty breeds poverty.

The 1960s was also the last time the federal government mean-
ingfully sought to eradicate poverty in the US. In January 1964,
just two months after he became president following the assassination of President John F. Kennedy, Lyndon Johnson delivered
his first State of the Union address as president. "This administration today, here and now, declares unconditional war on poverty
in America," he said. "It will not be a short or easy struggle, no
single weapon or strategy will suffice, but we shall not rest until
that war is won. The richest nation on Earth can afford to win it.
We cannot afford to lose it." All sorts of programs that we now
take for granted were launched: food stamps, now known as the
ever-under-assault Supplemental Nutrition Assistance Program

or SNAP; Medicare for senior citizens' health care; and Medicaid for the health care of poor people. The miracle of Head Start is responsible for higher reading and math scores and long-term educational and social benefits—more stable lives, steady employment, higher educational achievement—for children who attend the program. And Social Security benefits were expanded to include children and struggling families.

As he launched this war—the only successful one in his administration—Johnson and Lady Bird, his wife, traveled to Martin County, Kentucky, to show America what was at stake. Poverty in central Appalachia in 1960 was at 59 percent, and by visiting families mired in it, the president gave Congress compelling reason to vote for and fund the programs he hoped to enact. And yet, I did a double take when I read an article about the fiftieth anniversary of his visit. A reporter from *USA Today* retraced his steps and met a woman who was only six years old when Johnson visited, living in a shack with her parents and seventeen siblings. Their lot was somewhat improved, fifty years later, but not substantially. That little girl was now a fifty-five-year-old grandmother living in a two-bedroom trailer in rural Kentucky with her daughter and two grandchildren, all of whom receive food stamps and child support.

"We've progressed in certain areas," she said. "We do have things like indoor plumbing."

I will always believe that God led me back to Lowndes County, no matter all the twists and turns that my life might have taken before then. And the Lord gave me an opportunity to try to live his Word from the Gospel of Matthew 25:40: "Whatever you did for one of the least of these brothers and sisters of mine, you did for me."

When I became a consultant in economic development for Lowndes County in 2001, I was naive about the living conditions of my former neighbors—and this was a community I knew well. At the time, it seemed clear that economic development was the key to launching people out of poverty. I thought that if I succeeded in attracting investment to the area, all else would follow. Obviously, I did not fully appreciate that there was no viable infrastructure in this community to attract business, much less residents who could afford the goods and services businesses depended on. As I wrote in my first book, *Waste,* "We were between Selma and Montgomery, where throngs of well-meaning people passed each year to commemorate Dr. King's march. Yet along the route, folks were still living in third-world conditions, and nobody was fighting for them."

The following year, I was asked by a Lowndes County commissioner to visit a family who had been threatened with eviction and arrest because their septic system was not working and they couldn't afford to repair it. Only then did I discover one of the greatest injustices in our country and what became my calling.

Mattie and Odell McMeans lived in a trailer community with about eighteen family members dispersed among five trailers. Because of a failing septic system, raw sewage flowed from their home. The pastor from a small church in that community cried when he told us that his church had no septic tank at all and because of that he had been forbidden by local authorities to conduct services. Moreover, if he didn't fix the problem—at a cost of several thousand unaffordable dollars—he could be arrested. My home state criminalized the failure to provide a septic tank with punitive fines and possible imprisonment. Soon I discovered even more families faced this life-destroying dilemma.

I managed to bring this small catastrophe—but truly the canary in the coal mine—to the attention of Robert Woodson, the Black Republican head of the nonprofit Center for Neighborhood Enterprise (formerly called the National Center for Neighborhood Enterprise). He specialized in urban poverty—the seemingly intractable blight, with high unemployment, low investment, and embattled schools and streets. Some are encapsulated neighborhoods of major cities—the greater South Bronx in New York City, for example. Others are cities in themselves, like Flint, Michigan, or Jackson, Mississippi, where 28.9 percent of the residents have annual household incomes of less than $25,000. Woodson was a champion of what were known as "enterprise zones," a strategy of luring businesses into blighted neighborhoods with generous tax breaks and other incentives, with the idea that these businesses would serve as catalysts for uplifting the whole community. The National Historic Seaport in Baltimore is one example. But of course, gentrification often follows, and with it comes the displacement of the very residents these enterprise zones were designed to assist.

Because of my appeals, Woodson became interested in rural poverty. I invited him to Lowndes County, and he accepted. He was astonished by people living without sewers or septic tanks, with waste running into ditches alongside roads and in yards. He shared what he had seen with the *Washington Post* columnist William Raspberry, who wrote a column about Lowndes County that focused largely on the issue of sewage and high power bills but also touched on the bigger social problem of addressing rural poverty. He quoted Woodson's observations at length. He compared the situation in our community to a "virtual hurricane," saying that "if a real hurricane struck the area and wiped everything out, we would go in with engineers, builders, truckloads of septic tanks. The governor, volunteers, and the private sector would all come together to do what needed to be done."

Of course, that response never happened, although Woodson did stay engaged, bringing a number of high-profile and influential visitors to witness what was happening in Lowndes County firsthand. He connected us with Greg Snyder, an executive at HSBC bank who arranged support so that twenty homes either received new septic systems or had their existing ones repaired. Woodson was also an expert in playing the Washington, DC, game. As a Black conservative and an ardent Reagan supporter, he had made influential friends in the Republican party, among politicians and policymakers and in think tanks. He could see how their help could benefit everyone—from conservatives who, in their approaches to public policy, often were accused of disparaging the needs of poor people, not to mention poor Black people, to, frankly, the National Center for Neighborhood Enterprise itself, which could be seen as expanding its remit.

Because of people I met through Bob Woodson, I could see what poverty looked like in other parts of the country and how it affected white, Hispanic, and Indigenous people as well. My aperture widened beyond Lowndes, and I saw that this was a larger, systemic, and more pervasive problem. Whatever we could do to raise consciousness among people about the crisis of open sewage and the rural poor was what mattered most.

Fighting for sanitation justice seemed an unending job, and once I started in Lowndes County, I saw how widespread the problem was in rural communities throughout the South. What this battle revealed, however, was that the problem was much larger than septic systems. It cast an unforgiving spotlight on fundamental governance inadequacies and political disinterest in rural communities. Most elected officials and all but a few policy-makers have allowed rural communities to be isolated and die a slow and painful death—or become inundated with polluting plants owned by multinational corporations.

After all, the residents of these communities tend not to be par-ticularly politically active; indeed, they often are not even engaged until it is time to vote. No lucrative fundraisers are held there, and gerrymandering and isolation have diluted what voting blocs might have existed. Certainly, some churches make efforts to get out the vote, but the return on investment for major political parties is relatively low. For some lawmakers, this is just a sin of omission; they are truly oblivious to the suffering, and they stay that way. For others, it is a sin of commission; they may be aware but have decided for whatever reason to make other demands their priorities. Then there are those who don't even want to acknowledge that they are from these areas. Their shame about their humble origins—and many do feel shame—prevents them from doing anything about the problems. And so the cycle continues and the gap widens.

Many of the models for addressing the problem were created in universities and think tanks, but they have no real-world ap-plication on the ground. Occasionally, well-meaning consultants parachute in, but often they lack the curiosity to just . . . listen. In terms of arriving at solutions and balancing our common interests and providing support, we are not going to do that by relying on people whose only visits to rural communities have been random campaign stops, followed by speedy returns to the nation's capital, never experiencing the real-life implications of their policies.

As a trusted daughter of Lowndes County, I have also had the privilege of access to people in power: elected officials, public-interest leaders, national advocates, and the media. I have reached out to them and introduced them to my community, year after year, so they can see it firsthand, bridging the urban-rural divide. I have come to realize that doing this involves spanning political chasms as well. Party affiliations may be the way our increasingly polarized world organizes itself, but in order to advance toward productive change, those affiliations often get in the way. Whether or not your septic tank works when you flush a toilet is not a partisan political issue.

I FIRST MET ALABAMA SENATOR Jeff Sessions in 2002, in Fort Deposit, a town in Lowndes County. The two senators from Alabama would periodically hold town hall–like meetings where they would brief their constituents on what was going on in Washington, DC. I decided to attend one for myself and ask a few questions. The setting was the small auditorium of the local National Guard armory. I don't think it held more than two hundred people, and it wasn't crowded. When I looked at the gathering, I saw that white men—businessmen and farmers—comprised the bulk of the audience.

Senator Sessions described new efforts the federal government had launched to help rural communities, all of which required about a 25 percent local match. He appeared to be very optimistic about the possibilities that this offered, but I could not help but see the initiative's fatal flaw. During the question-and-answer period, I raised my hand. How was this possible, I asked, when poor counties have virtually no tax base from which to fund that match? He gave me a very thoughtful reply, acknowledging that he too struggled to reconcile this problem. And then he added, "I grew up poor in Wilcox County." I knew Wilcox County well. Adjacent to Lowndes County and located in the Black Belt, it shares the same issues regarding sanitation and rural poverty.

In the wake of this town hall, I had an audacious idea to attract political attention. Two thousand two was an election year and Senator Sessions was running for his second term. Alabama can be pretty fickle with its senators, and no Republican had ever been reelected to a second full term. So, a few months later, I enlisted the help of a local businessman and arranged a fundraiser for Sessions in Lowndes County. Nearly ten thousand people live there, and, according to the most recent census, 73 percent are Black and about 25 percent are white; 83 percent graduated from high school, while only 17 percent have college degrees. The median household income is $33,125. Nearly 30 percent of the residents live below the poverty line. Still, there were businesses in this community and some well-off Black residents who were pleased to host the visit of a sitting US senator. I met Senator Sessions at an event earlier that evening, and together we went to the fundraiser. During our drive, he asked me what I wanted. My answer was simple: "I want help for Lowndes County."

He listened. Senator Sessions sent members of his staff to Lowndes County and to our public hearings elsewhere in the state, as well as to our meetings with state officials. His staff also were dismayed by the level of poverty and neglect in which residents lived, and they committed to addressing the problem.

Soon, such an opportunity appeared: I asked Senator Sessions if he could put pressure on the EPA to release funding for a stalled federal appropriation for sewage treatment. Later the same year, we became the only poor community to receive EPA funding for a national demonstration project, an opportunity to create a program and try it out on a local level as a way to determine if it might be potentially replicable on a bigger scale. In our case, the project involved economic development in a poor community with the intention to remedy the sanitation crisis.

Understanding that decent jobs could offer another path to functioning sanitation, when Hyundai built a huge manufacturing plant in a neighboring county, just six miles from Lowndes County, Senator Sessions also secured $4 million in grants from the Department of Commerce to construct industrial parks. The opening of the Interpretive Center in Lowndes County, a site that commemorates the historic events associated with the 1965 voting-rights marches, was accompanied by some terrible racist attacks. Some of Sessions's constituents no doubt assumed he would sympathize with the attackers, but in fact it was quite the reverse. The senator and I toured the exhibits. "Everyone should know this history," he said quietly.

When President Donald Trump nominated Senator Sessions as his first attorney general, the vitriol directed against him was relentless. He was accused of terrible racism and pilloried for his record on civil rights when he was a lawyer and as Alabama attorney general. In 1986, Sessions was a US attorney in Alabama and had been nominated to the federal judiciary, a position that required being confirmed by the US Senate. At his confirmation hearing, several people spoke up and described troubling incidents. One of them was Thomas Figures, a Black assistant US attorney who'd worked for him, who told the Senate Judiciary Committee that Sessions had called him "boy" several times. He also said that, for Sessions, the Ku Klux Klan was just the punch line of a joke. Sessions allegedly had said that he had thought there was nothing wrong with Klan members, Figures said, "until he learned that they smoked marijuana."

Figures and J. Gerald Herbert, who was a Department of Justice lawyer at the time, both described Sessions making disparaging comments about civil rights groups. Sessions reportedly had referred to the NAACP, the Southern Christian Leadership Conference, Operation PUSH, and the National Council of Churches as "un-American organizations teaching anti-American values." Sessions, who denied all the allegations strenuously, even describing them as "heartbreaking," never became a federal judge; the Judiciary Committee voted 10–8 against his nomination. Naturally, these accusations were revived after his nomination to US attorney general.

I wrote a friend, "I have been seeing all the press on Senator Sessions, and I do not recognize the person they're describing. From my vantage point, I don't know who he may have been at

one time, but I have known him to be a friend to the people of
Lowndes County."

As an Alabama native, I have watched the career of Tommy
Tuberville for over twenty-five years. His career coaching the
Auburn University football team from 1999 to 2008 almost par-
alleled my own work in the state. I returned to Lowndes after
several years away, most recently teaching in Detroit. I decided
to come back home after my father died on March 28, 2000. I saw
a real opportunity to take what I had learned about community
organizing and education and apply those lessons toward improving the lives of those closest to me. When I returned to Alabama,
Selma was trying to elect its first Black mayor, James Perkins, and
I was hired by the NAACP to work on the Voter Empowerment
Project to help secure his victory.

Being back in Alabama meant many things to me, including
a return to the world of college football. During that time, there
were few conversations about college football that did not include
the ascent of Tommy Tuberville. Over his career, Tuberville sent
twenty-nine players to the NFL. He defeated Auburn's greatest
rival, the Crimson Tide from the University of Alabama, six times
in a row and boasted an undefeated 2004 season. He may have
gone on to coach in Texas and Ohio after his time at Auburn, but
Alabamans have always considered him one of our own. No one
was surprised when he returned to the state to run for office. In
2020, a year when Democrats swept the House and Senate, his
decisive victory was a rare bright spot for Republicans when he
became the junior senator representing the state. Meanwhile, my

own reputation and mission had grown, and I had become much more engaged on a national level.

On July 19, 2023, I was invited to testify at a Senate subcommittee hearing on "Rural Water: Modernizing Our Community Water Systems" by the Agriculture, Nutrition, and Forestry committee chairman, Vermont senator Peter Welch. My work had been brought to his attention by New Jersey senator Cory Booker, whom I had gotten to know years before when he was the first US senator outside of Alabama to visit with my organization, the Center for Rural Enterprise and Environmental Justice, in Lowndes County. Senator Tuberville was the ranking member on the committee, and I was one of the experts called upon to discuss the challenges many communities face in accessing clean water and effective sanitation.

Before the hearing got underway, I decided to introduce myself to Senator Tuberville. At the time, he was holding up the promotion of military officers to protest a Department of Defense policy that provided funding and support for service members seeking abortions. As someone from a military family, I knew what a profound and negative impact his unilateral freeze had on the lives of servicepeople, and how important it was for all women to have access to reproductive health care. Senator Tuberville had also been presented as someone who might very well be antagonistic toward me, given the organizations with which I was affiliated, like the Natural Resources Defense Council, which had been demonized by many conservatives because of its environmental advocacy. And yet, I also knew that he was someone who had engaged in deep conversations with many Black mothers, as he discussed their sons' football careers. I wondered if this meant he had a level of comfort in connecting with Black women that other white law-makers did not.

I knew when I walked into the room that I was there to advocate on behalf of rural communities; he knew that these were his constituents, some of the voters who had put him in office. I walked up and extended my hand, and after a brief exchange of pleasantries I got to the point. "Senator, I believe that when a homeowner buys a septic tank, the liability should not automatically be transferred to them," I said. "They should come with ten-year warranties because otherwise, poor people who live in rural communities will suffer."

He not only agreed with me; he understood that if manufacturers faced no liability, it placed needy consumers—all consumers really—on a collision course with a failing system that they couldn't afford to repair. Plus, there was no incentive for manufacturers to improve their products. He put his arm around me and asked me to turn toward an official Senate photographer holding a camera so she could record the moment. He assured me that his Huntsville office would be in touch. I took my seat. There were five of us providing testimony that day, two who'd been chosen by the Republicans on the committee and three chosen by Democrats. I found myself sitting in the middle, between the two sides.

In my remarks to the committee, I outlined the problem: "According to the Census Bureau's American Housing Survey, 18 percent of all US households—about one in five homes—are not able to send their sewage to be treated by a centralized waste-water system. About twenty-two million households use a decentralized wastewater system such as a septic tank or cesspool; 180,000 households use rudimentary sewage-disposal approaches like outhouses and chemical toilets; and 35,000 households have no form of wastewater treatment at all."

I spoke about Centreville, Illinois, and Mount Vernon, New York. I talked about Appalachia and Puerto Rico, and how colonias and tribal nations in the Southwest disproportionately lack indoor plumbing. I told them that sanitation systems are absent or failing in small, rural communities from California's Central Valley to native villages in Alaska. I asked for a more robust database tracking the status of unsewered households nationwide and urged lawmakers to consider the importance of extending centralized sewers to households who lacked them. And I pointed out that funding innovation was key, noting that NASA had done more research than either the EPA or USDA on addressing this most basic of human needs.

As the subcommittee hearing unfolded, whatever apprehension I may have felt beforehand vanished. This was where the real work of Congress took place. Away from cameras and gavel-to-gavel coverage, here was a rare moment of solidarity, where people on both sides of the aisle agreed that this was an issue that needed to be addressed. We were talking to each other, rather than railing against each other.

The work of Congress is often invisible and certainly glacial, but somehow it seemed as if things were moving in the right direction. First, I received a couple of text messages from Senator Booker's office after the hearing, and he seemed pleased that there was an unusual level of bipartisan support for addressing the wastewater problem. Then in October, I learned that Senator Booker was working with Senator Tuberville, trying to get the funding for wastewater grants increased in the 2024 US Farm Bill from $5 million to $20 million, but in the final bill, unfortunately, it was only increased by $1 million. The significance here is that a progressive senator and an extreme right-wing senator worked together in common cause for rural sanitation. At the time of this writing, it remains to be seen how the states will decide to distribute their funds to historically underserved communities like Lowndes County.

What was especially exciting for me was to see that another government agency, the EPA, made an effort to close the wastewater-access gap, and this time Lowndes County was specifically mentioned. My community was awarded a 100 percent forgivable loan of $8.7 million to address failing or nonexistent wastewater systems in 650 homes. Could I trace this success directly back to that hearing in July? Of course, so many other political factors were involved in making this happen. But what was clear was that every once in a while, it is possible to bridge a political divide.

WE DON'T HAVE TO LOOK FAR into history to see what a fully mobilized, multidimensional effort to eradicate poverty might look like. My parents were both born during the Great Depression: my father in 1930 when it began and my mother in 1939 when the alphabet soup of New Deal programs had eased some but far from all of the suffering. No one was spared in the economic collapse. Meanwhile, the details of individual lives still have the power to shock. The lucky coal miners who were still employed made one dollar a day. Milk was eliminated from children's diets, and many were so hungry, so ill, and had so few clothes that school became a distant memory. Horses were still a form of transportation for many rural people, and they often dropped dead from starvation. Figuring out a place to work was much more urgent—but where? Much has been written about the vast dimensions of hardship inflicted by the Great Depression, but one thing stands out to me: the South had an extra dose of suffering.

Even during a time of catastrophic national unemployment, poverty, and hardship, Alabama's misery was notable. The state had the highest unemployment rate in the South. Per capita, no other city lost as many jobs as Birmingham. Before the Depression, one hundred thousand people had full-time employment there; after the crash, only fifteen thousand people had jobs. In 1929, the annual income for an average Alabama family was $311; six years later, it was $194. Historian David M. Kennedy in his book *Freedom from Fear: The American People in Depression and War, 1929–1945* quoted the observations of Lorena Hickok, a newspaper reporter who was close with Eleanor Roosevelt, as she traveled through the South in the midst of the catastrophe. She wrote that Southern farm workers were "half-starved Whites and Blacks [who] struggle in competition for less to eat than my dog gets at home, for the privilege of living in huts that are infinitely less comfortable than his kennel."

These demographic realities, however, ignore some of the human realities on the ground. In Lowndes County, where my family lived, the Depression was not the cataclysmic event that divided life dramatically between a time of prosperity and a time of poverty. People here had always lived modestly. They had each other and they had land. They had the skills they needed to survive: emotional ones like resilience, determination, and self-reliance, and practical ones like canning, cultivating small gardens, and sharing what little they had, because when everyone shared, everyone had more. These strategies and gifts were developed over years of being a Black person in the South.

My family was never swept into what was known as the "Great Migration," a period in the 1920s when 750,000 African Americans in the South moved to northern and western cities to escape the oppressive systemic racism and terror of Jim Crow. Even without the dangers of lynching, indignities organized every aspect of daily life for a Black person: Segregation in schools, workplaces, and public buildings, including shops and restaurants. Impassable barriers to voting. Soaring infant mortality rates and unreachable health care. A racist justice system, from sheriffs in the smallest hamlets to the state supreme courts, in which anything resembling a fair trial for a Black person was impossible. In the 1930s, the Black population of America was concentrated in the South, where four out of five African Americans lived. Interestingly, when the economic miseries from the Great Depression took hold in northern cities, a small "reverse" migration took place, with some Black families returning to the South under the assumption that they would at least be able to grow some food to survive. Too often, they were wrong.

Both my parents' families remained in Alabama—my mother's family in Autauga County and my father's in Lowndes. They never referred to stories from the Depression, since I suppose the deprivation then was not measurably different from the deprivation that was a fact of their lives. Most important, they knew how to prosper in adversity, which made them more resilient when the cataclysm struck the nation.

Even though they were just children when Franklin Delano Roosevelt was president, my parents revered him and would continue to do so, long after his death. In the summer of 1932, when Roosevelt appeared at the Democratic National Convention to accept the nomination, he famously said, "I pledge to you, I pledge to myself, a New Deal for the American people." His first hundred days in office involved a breathtaking series of legislative victories designed to provide immediate relief to Americans. Fifteen major bills were passed; one created the Civilian Conservation Corps to put unemployed men back to work planting trees, bolstering national parks, and fighting forest fires. Eventually 2.5 million men were employed. The Public Works Administration, part of the National Industrial Recovery Act, channeled government money into state infrastructure projects like roads and bridges. With the Homeowners Refinancing Act, people in danger of losing their homes were given low-interest loans and refinancing options. What FDR managed to do was give American citizens a jolt of self-confidence after years of despair.

Alabama, still mostly dependent on the cash crop of cotton as its economic engine, had been in dire economic straits for years. For Black people—many of them illiterate—agriculture was where they found work, along with all the uncertainties and vulnerabilities that came with it. Few Black people owned the land they farmed, and in Alabama, sharecroppers both white and Black worked three-quarters of the land, which meant none of them had autonomy or a sense of security about their homes or livelihood. Even in the 1920s, sharecroppers began to experience how imperiled their circumstances were. Cotton crops had been devastated by a boll weevil infestation, and international competition drove cotton prices so low that owners of cotton farms passed their losses down to the people who worked the land. When the stock market crashed in 1929, the state's economy was already in a perilous condition.

During the Depression, 65 percent of all farmers were tenant farmers, and 39 percent of tenant farmers were sharecroppers. Tenant farmers might own their own equipment or supplies—although they were still utterly dependent on the landlords—but sharecroppers didn't own anything they might need for farming, and neither tenant farmers nor sharecroppers had any claim at all on the land they farmed. In both cases, white owners charged them for equipment, as well as basic necessities, such as tools, food, clothing, and seed at stores also owned by whites. An unbroken cycle of debt and dependence was thereby created, and a circumstance known as "debt peonage," which Congress banned after the Civil War (but which never really disappeared), returned with a vengeance. Workers could hardly avoid falling behind on payments for necessities, so then liens were placed on their crops, depriving them of the only available means for paying off their ever-mounting debt. Farm income in Alabama plummeted by more than 30 percent from 1930 to 1933 because the farms produced too much cotton, which they were unable to sell, leading to greater debt, greater scarcity, and sometimes eviction from the properties that the sharecroppers or tenant farmers may not have owned but had worked on for generations. Overall, historians have noted that the effects of the Depression in Alabama started earlier and lasted longer than in other parts of the country.

Still, there were ways for some to markedly improve their lives, namely the military and education. With the mandatory draft, even though the military was still segregated, many men—and even women—enlisted. By 1927, there were seventy-seven HBCUs, educating almost fourteen thousand students. Many of these institutions are in the South, and fifteen of the most notable—Tuskegee, Alabama A&M, Alabama State University, Oakwood University, and Stillman, among them—are located in Alabama, which has the most HBCUs of any state. Through donations from churches, philanthropies, and prosperous Black communities, these places of higher education not only survived; they thrived during those dark years. The Department of Education notes that enrollment during this period grew by 60 percent, and it grew still more after the war, when the GI Bill paid college tuition and expenses for returning veterans.

Slowly, throughout the country, a fragile optimism returned for some. Others were appalled at Roosevelt's efforts and thought he was pushing the country toward socialism. But it was during this time that my family, like others, secured their land. The Agricultural Adjustment Act favored white landowners, and when there were funds to be distributed, they went through previously existing white groups in rural communities, which naturally passed them along to other white people. Even as farmland dropped in value, Black farmers found it difficult to access the funding needed to purchase it, while white farmers and even tenant farmers increased their ownership. And yet, over that period of time, about 219,000 Black farmers who had been sharecroppers came to own their land, and that land wealth boosted them into the middle or upper-middle classes. Many of them went on to become leaders in their communities.

A program created in the mid-1930s as part of the Farm Security Administration was designed to help tenants gain independence as farmers. It involved subdividing massive tracts of land, usually former plantations, and offering subsidies to Black farmers so they could purchase these parcels. This is how my father's great-grandparents were able to buy their land. One of the most notable land purchases was in Macon County, Alabama, about two hours east of Lowndes County, where, in partnership with the Tuskegee Institute, a community known as Prairie Farms was created out of two former plantations. The plan, organized entirely by African American managers, was to have impoverished Black families from the Black Belt relocate to Prairie Farms. The community had a utopian flavor, with family homes, all of which had septic systems and a cooperative system for farm equipment and marketing of the crops. A kindergarten-through-twelfth-grade school offered hot lunches for students and became a hub for community meetings, health care, adult education classes, and even plays. But World War II put an end to this kind of idealism; the country had other demands to attend to.

I must admit, I feel some nostalgia for a time when there was such a commitment by our government to lifting up lives that had been beaten down. The historian David Kennedy described the legacy of the New Deal in a way that feels even more timely today: "Above all, the New Deal gave to countless Americans who had never had much of it a sense of security, and with it a sense of having a stake in their country. And it did it all without shredding the American constitution or sundering the American people. At a time when despair and alienation were prostrating other peoples under the heel of dictatorship, that was no small accomplishment."

So often when I visit poor communities—and this is true of urban areas as well as rural ones—the feeling of "despair and alienation" is so powerful. One of the well-known paradoxes of our interconnected world, where information is so immediately accessible and social networks pretend to create community, is that people feel more divided, more isolated, and often more anxious and depressed than ever before. The time when my grandparents and their children would sit and listen to the reassuring voice of President Roosevelt over the radio is in the very distant past. Behind that voice, however, was real action, a real recognition that it was the responsibility of the government to address problems and make the lives of individual Americans better. In helping one person's life to improve, the lives of others could improve as well. Yes, those times are long gone. But the need for hope in a better future remains. And life has shown me that hope can sometimes appear in the most unlikely places.

In 2019, in the lead-up to the presidential election, the only candidate to visit Lowndes County was Vermont senator Bernie Sanders. When his staff first contacted me to see if he could make a brief stop, I told them that wasn't going to happen. No one can drop into a community where rural people live and assume it's okay to shake a few hands and leave. That might work in large cities, where there are so many people and everyone is in a rush and there is a need to see and be seen. But in a small, poor community— a small, poor, rural Southern community at that—the most basic show of respect requires one to pause, look, and listen. And that takes time.

To my surprise, rather than brush us off, Senator Sanders, a democratic socialist who has been the longest-serving independent during his nearly thirty years in Congress, was willing to take the time. We met in Lowndes County, and I took him to visit my old friend Pamela Rush, who lived in a double-wide trailer with straight-pipe plumbing, which meant that the sewage in her home drained directly under the collapsed deck and into her backyard. Her home was falling apart, with the ceiling buckling and opossums and other wild animals setting up house in the holes in her walls. She had less than $1,000 a month to support her two children, one of whom suffered from asthma. The interest rate on her trailer, which she bought in 1995, was 10 percent. Twenty-four years later, she still owed $13,000 on it. Since the state took no responsibility for her sewage, installing a system would have easily cost her more than $20,000.

When Senator Sanders visited, he was visibly shocked. He took his time, staying awhile to speak with Pamela's children. Then he spoke quietly to Pamela. He tried to reassure her that something would be done, that she was not alone. "The truth is that in America today, we have many, many millions of people who are spending 40 to 50 to 60 percent of their limited incomes on housing," he told reporters who had traveled with him, unwittingly echoing the words of Lyndon Johnson sixty years earlier. "These types of conditions should not be existing in the wealthiest nation in the history of the world."

In a campaign video entitled "Trapped," he reflected on his visit: "When we use the expression 'It is very expensive to be poor,' this is what we're talking about. The word *poverty* is something that is not talked about very often in the United States. We have tens of millions of people in the richest country in the world who are struggling every single day to care for their families in the most basic way."

Less than a year later, when the coronavirus pandemic ripped through the world, other consequences of this neglect were thrust into the foreground. As a community where most people did not have the luxury of working from home to survive and had to go to the stores or factories or nursing homes that employed them, Lowndes County soon had the highest per capita death rate in the state. One invisible human story embedded in those grim statistics was that of Pamela Rush, who ended up dying alone in the intensive care unit at the University of Alabama's Birmingham Medical Center. The official cause of death was COVID, but the underlying causes of her suffering were poverty, environmental injustice, climate change, race, and health disparities. These would never be listed on a death certificate.

"There but for the grace of God go I" is the famous paraphrase of what the apostle Paul said in Corinthians 15:10. I wonder sometimes, with so many deeply religious lawmakers out there, how many take to heart those simple words. How many people take the time to truly see these unassuming lives? These are people whose grandparents and great-grandparents were likely grateful for any New Deal program that promised to improve their lives. Who knows what talents their children might bring into the world, if only given a chance? Who knows what contributions they could have made, were they not invisible and ignored?

There they are, out of sight for most Americans because it seems the gulf is too vast, the gap seemingly unbridgeable. Politicians, of course, respond to and reflect what they perceive to be the preoccupations and concerns of the greatest number of voters in their particular districts. I suppose that makes it easy to explain why our rural poor are too often overlooked by our elected officials, are too often not a part of the national conversation. Yes, there are some moments like the one that took place in a small hearing room on Capitol Hill, or when a politician comes to visit a poor community. So I feel—I must feel—some hope. After all, my life's work is predicated on my belief that this is a gap that can be bridged, and part of my mission on Earth is to act as that bridge.

When I was a teacher, I used to have a book about building character that I shared with my students. It was a collection of uplifting stories about becoming a person with integrity—and how character is a quality that does not just magically appear but must be nurtured and built with patience and attention. One of the stories that still stays with me was about a stone maker who confronted an enormous boulder. Day by day, he patiently chipped away at the stone, until slowly his patience was rewarded and a beautiful sculpture emerged, as if it had just been waiting for someone like him to do the work. The story was so meaningful to me, in its lessons about tenacity and dedication. But it also contains a message that could go far in bridging so many divides in our country: contained in something that appears ugly and forbidding, great beauty may reside.

THREE

Food for the Soul

THE BACK SEAT OF THE ENORMOUS BLACK CADILLAC
Escalade has plenty of space, with an almost new-car-clean smell
and easily accessible small bottles of water. Once we settle in, we
have the sense of being cared for, with just a little bit of luxury.
My speaker's bureau had engaged a limo service to drive me
from Huntsville, where I live, to Auburn, where I have some
speaking engagements. Auburn is one of Alabama's largest universities, with nearly thirty thousand students, a powerhouse
football team, and a former football coach who is now a sitting
US senator. Depending on the traffic, the 245-mile drive mostly
down I-65 from Huntsville to Auburn takes about three and
a half hours. If I had a nickel for every time I've been on that
road, I would be a wealthy woman. My thoughts go to the busy
schedule ahead: first, a reception before my school-wide lecture

that evening, then the two classes I'm scheduled to teach the day after. One is a journalism class and the other is a sociology course about research methods.

Two friends have joined me for the excursion, and our driver, who I'll call Toby, is a white country boy from Alabama, all grown up, in a dark suit, tie, and a white shirt. Both my friends are from the North, but Lynda, who is Black, moved from Pittsburgh to Montgomery, Alabama, several years ago and now lives in Huntsville. She's gotten to know the state, and the experience of being a Black woman in the South, very well. Toby grew up in the Alabama countryside and still lives there, not far from Auburn. He's a man who knows rural poverty, though likely would never use those words to describe his past. He reminisces about the Black woman, his "auntie," who watched him after school and would sometimes send home food. He tells Lynda about the church he attends and churches he has rejected.

My other friend, who is white, has spent little time in the South. It's her first trip to Alabama, so as we rocket down the highway, we point out a few landmarks on the way. How the mountains around Huntsville give way farther south to flatter land, good for cultivation. How the next time she visits, we might spend some time in Birmingham and see the sights she only knows from history books on the Civil Rights Movement—the Sixteenth Street Baptist Church, for example, or the Bethel Baptist Church, or Kelly Ingram Park, where those involved with the Southern Christian Leadership Conference gathered with activists from other groups. "When you come back," I say as we pass an exit sign, "we'll figure out a way to spend some time there." She heartily agrees.

So, the miles drift by. Sometimes there are parallel conversations going on in the front and the back seats. Sometimes the conversations crisscross. Lynda and Toby exchange observations about gas mileage, and in the back we discuss DNA testing, and I describe some of the ancestors I've found. There are companionable silences too, when we check our phones or just stare out the window as we draw closer to our first destination. Lunchtime is approaching, and we plan to stop at Davis Café, which is known to have the best soul food in Montgomery, ever since the place first opened in 1988. And I find myself thinking random thoughts about a subject with which I've been preoccupied recently.

"Have you ever noticed," I say to no one in particular, breaking a silence that has settled in, "that food just doesn't seem to smell as good as it did in the past?"

It is as if I have thrown open a door and let in a blast of invigorating fresh air. Everyone has thoughts to share.

"That's right!" Toby says with the joy of connecting over a common problem. "You can't smell the fried chicken the same way as when we were kids."

I like that he includes me in his generation, even though I am old enough to be his mother. But I'm glad that he agrees. And all of a sudden, all these insights and feelings and memories just tumble out of us.

"I remember when I was a child, the happiest times of the year were around Thanksgiving and Christmas," I say. "I miss my parents especially during those holidays. My mother would make caramel cake. . . ."

"Oh my God," Toby says. "My grandma made caramel cake—it was her specialty. I mean, she made it for every occasion—birthdays, funerals, new babies. . . ."

Caramel cakes may sound foreign to some people—as they did to my friend from up North—but if you are from the South, they are part of the culinary landscape at important family and community events: weddings, baptisms, funerals, church suppers. It's basically a yellow layer cake, but the magic of it comes from the singular rich and buttery caramel frosting that gives it its name. It apparently originated in the Mississippi Delta, a region where a fruit tree is nearly impossible to find but where sugar cane is abundant. In some families, the recipe was written down, but mostly it was passed from great-grandmother to grandmother to mother to daughter. The special challenge is the caramel icing, which can go wrong in inexperienced hands, becoming too sticky, too drippy, or too granular. It's a cake that is more than just a cake, as is apparent from how our conversation turns into something like a call and response in church as we share memories of caramel cakes in our lives.

"Mama used to make it from scratch. . . ."

"She used Pet milk, butter, sugar, and vanilla extract. You remember Pet milk?"

"*Of course* I remember Pet milk."

"You just *had* to use that for the caramel cake. Sure, you could try some of that sweetened condensed milk, but it just didn't do what it was supposed to do."

"Did you get the recipe?"

"She never used any recipes. My grandma made it during Christmas seasons."

"That's how I learned to make biscuits, from my grandma. You take everything in your hands, and use lard, but *not* Crisco—"

"Never Crisco."

"Lard in the box, the white box we got from the government."

"Or a green box, from the store. Armour lard—"

"Slow down!" I interrupted. "My mother used Crisco for her biscuits! We had lard in a can, not a box, so they could strain it and reuse it."

"Yeah, I still see that green box of lard. And we strained the fat too, into an old coffee can. . . ."

"Wait a minute, Davis Café is on North Decatur, isn't it? We're almost there."

FOOD DEFINES US. Food nourishes us. Food delights us. Food can sometimes disappoint us. Food engages all our senses and embeds in our memories. And yet, as I try to recall just how my mother's perfect sweet potato pie tasted and smelled, long after she has passed, the experience feels *almost* accessible but just out of reach. Sometimes, unpredictably, I catch a scent that transports me back to a time when my family was all together around the table, digging into that pie and trading stories. But the experience is so fleeting, it almost feels as if it couldn't have happened. I spend so much time looking at the problems we face with disposing of waste from one end that I can't ignore what's happening at the other.

Food is celebratory, it's comforting, and it's conciliatory; it can sicken us and sustain us. In his seminal 1943 paper on human motivation, American psychologist Abraham Maslow laid out a pyramid that depicted a hierarchy of needs. At the bottom of the pyramid were the foundational physiological needs of food, air, water, shelter, clothing, and sleep, all but one of which we share with the rest of the animal kingdom. But as humans, our relationship to food is vast and complicated. It is social as well as biological. Sharing a meal connects us in ways nothing else can. It can bridge gaps among people of very different backgrounds and experiences. It can be a source of torment and dysfunction, of joy and memory. And while every generation devises its own special relationship with what they eat, as I mentioned on our trip to Auburn, what we are eating, and often the way we are eating it, seems to have lost some essential and important qualities.

Why do some eating experiences stick with us, while others disappear? In 2015, I was in France for the first time. I'm sure that I had a number of fantastic meals, but one in particular stands out in my memory. We were at a restaurant that served us a whole fish. Now, I have eaten an aquarium full of fish over the years, but nothing like this—so beautifully seasoned, I could taste the fish and the sea from which it came. In my mind, I still can. Several years later, I visited a small town called Erlach, almost two hours outside of Geneva, Switzerland, and my friends took me to Pizzeria Margherita, a local Italian restaurant owned by a Croatian refugee whose family had moved to Italy during the Bosnian war in the 1990s. She served a salad in a mason jar. It was filled with the freshest vegetables—carrots and tomatoes, greens and cucumbers—and every vegetable's flavor was distinct, as if it were the original creation after which all others were modeled. Blended together, it made them unlike anything that I had ever experienced.

Having lived in Detroit, with its jigsaw puzzle of ethnic neighborhoods, I understood how important food was to cultural identity. In Hamtramck I enjoyed *paczki*, the famous Polish pastry, their yeasted version of a jelly doughnut—filled with prune or custard or lemon, my favorites. *Paczkis* are the Polish Mardi Gras treat, served on the Tuesday before Ash Wednesday and the fasting that begins during Lent. Then there were the treats in Greek Town—the honey-drenched walnut pastry, baklava, or the wonderful lemon, chicken, and rice avgolemono soup.

Consuming ethnic food in Detroit was a different experience from the one I had when I was living in Washington, DC, in the late 1980s. I attended Allen Chapel, an AME church known as "the Cathedral of the Southeast," on Sundays. They were renovating the main sanctuary at the time so early morning services were held at 8:00 a.m. One of the major attractions that kept me going to that service, other than the Word, was the aroma of breakfast food that drifted into our worship. We smelled coffee and bacon, fried ham, and biscuits, and any thoughts I might have had of leaving right after services disappeared. Our breakfasts there were not just mouthwatering gastronomic experiences; sharing food with others created a special sense of community. That food reminded me of the breakfasts of my childhood.

My mother was a very smart woman who worked full-time in order to feed five children and her husband. I am reminded of a remarkable interview with the Queen of Soul, Aretha Franklin. The interviewer asked her what she felt was the greatest challenge she'd faced in her life. He was probably expecting her to reflect on racism in American society or the difficulty of being a female R & B performer coming up in her generation. After pausing a few beats, she replied, "The greatest challenge in my life is what to cook for dinner, nightly, you know? Just night after night. What is it going to be tonight?"

The interviewer—a man, of course—laughed incredulously. "You don't actually *cook* your own dinner, do you?"

"Oh, please," she said. "I do my own washing, my own cooking, my own ironing, all of that."

Another lame protest from the questioner: How was it possible that a woman of her stature, a multiplatinum recording artist, would be trapped in the drudgery of women everywhere?

The Queen was having none of it. "You have to figure, what's it gonna be tonight? I did that last night," she said calmly, as if chatting over coffee at a kitchen table with a friend. "That's the hardest thing right there."

She could have been my mother and every mother, nearly every woman I know. Night after night my mother fed us, and she fed us well. Like everyone in our community, she had a big garden with corn and collard greens, tomatoes, and peppers and in the summer, a watermelon patch. When we lived in Montgomery, we could throw corn seeds out the back door and soon enough little plants started to grow. With such a big family, and with money being tight, birthday celebrations never included purchased gifts, but the birthday boy or girl received the best present of all: we could order our favorite meal for dinner. Mine was fried chicken breasts and greens. Since there were seven people in our house, when we had chicken, a single bird had to be divided among many people. Our parents would have the breasts, and the rest of us would enjoy the wings, thighs, legs—except on my birthday, when my mother would happily present me with my special gift.

I never knew my mother's mother. She died when my mother was only a teenager. But my father's mother was a very powerful presence in our lives, and Sunday dinners at her house in Birmingham were events many people looked forward to. She loved to cook—especially big meals on Sunday—and a few country boys from Lowndes County who were working in Birmingham would often come to her house to eat. They wanted a meal that reminded them of home, and they got it. She would cook whatever she was in the mood to create that day, whether it was pork chops and gravy, fried chicken, rice and beans, fried corn with tomatoes, scalloped potatoes, fried okra, corn bread, red velvet cake, or sweet potato pie. Her table overflowed with delicious food. Plus, she would pick muscadine grapes and make her own wine—cooking them until they reached a boil, putting in a little sugar, and letting the mixture ferment before she strained it into mason jars.

People from rural communities have a special understanding of the value of mason jars. Like most Southern women, my grandmother would preserve fruit and vegetables for the winter. My mother would cut up peppers and put them in one of those jars with her own concoction of vinegar and salt and some sugar, maybe some hot peppers, for a great relish. And naturally, everything that was cooked or grown or preserved served our friends and neighbors too. Nobody had much, but everyone shared. You didn't visit someone without being pressed to take something they'd grown, cooked, or made.

As a child, I remember aromas from the neighbors' cooking wafting through the air, so it seemed possible while walking down the dirt road to imagine each individual dinner table as families sat down to eat. Today, I find fewer opportunities to make those kinds of memories. What has happened to the richly textured smells that food once carried: the perfume of peaches, the tang of a cut tomato, the bite of greens? There was a time when every family had a garden and exchanging produce was an expression of hospitality. Today, many of these same communities are food deserts, further examples of environmental injustice.

"WELL, HERE WE ARE," Toby announces as he pulls into the parking lot. He's like a kid who cannot believe his good luck in getting to go to an amusement park during a school day. His enthusiasm is understandable. Davis Café and Restaurant, whose tagline is "Home cooking at its best," is known throughout Montgomery—probably throughout Alabama—as the place for people who are longing for classic, even legendary soul food. George and Josie Davis opened their café and restaurant thirty-five years ago, and it still remains in the family; their granddaughter Sheila is in charge now. Over the years, when civil rights icons like Georgia congressman John R. Lewis, Rev. Dr. Joseph Lowery, Rev. Jesse Jackson, and Dr. Julian Bond, or musicians like Lil Wayne and Al Green were in the neighborhood and hungry, they were sure to visit Davis Café.

It's located not far from a part of Montgomery known as Old Alabama Town, a stretch of a few blocks with restored buildings from the nineteenth century, and just minutes from the Dexter Avenue Baptist Church. That's where, in 1955, the yearlong, transformative Montgomery bus boycott was launched. The church was the nerve center of the Civil Rights Movement, home to the young, brilliant pastor Dr. Martin Luther King Jr. He arrived the year of the landmark 1954 Supreme Court case *Brown v. Board of Education of Topeka, Kansas*—a crucial period of time for the movement. The ruling, which affirmed that race-based segregation of public schools violated the Fourteenth Amendment and was unconstitutional, memorialized the fact that there was no such thing as "separate but equal." Many tripwires set the movement in motion, but this was a crucial one, and a year later, the Montgomery bus boycott began, all planned in the basement of Reverend King's church. He only resigned in 1960, he later wrote, because "a multiplicity of new responsibilities poured in upon me in almost staggering torrents. So, I ended up futilely attempting to be four or five men in one."

Times have definitely changed, but the food that nourished the early civil rights leaders is part of the same tradition the Davis Café specializes in today. Admittedly the outside of the café could probably use a coat of paint, but the interior is spacious and nicely lit, nothing fancy of course. We walk into the large dining area and sit down at a square table. The menu changes every day, and since we arrive on a Thursday, they don't offer the turkey and dressing I had hoped for, so instead I go for the vegetables: collard greens, beans, rutabagas, fried okra, and cornbread. But there is so much to choose from—the fried chicken, fried steak, pot roast, turnip and mustard greens, breaded, fried okra, broccoli with cheese sauce—although they are out of the fresh peas and beans. Some of us order sweet tea, others unsweetened; both are available. Toby orders pot roast with potatoes and carrots smothered in gravy and three sides, all of which he devours. Lynda decides on the pot roast with rice and gravy. My Northern friend chooses the fried chicken and proceeds to eat it with a knife and fork. Lynda and I exchange a quick glance, and Lynda can't help herself. "Look at the way she's eating!" she says, laughing. The only way to eat fried chicken is as it always has been eaten—with your bare hands. My friend smiles and grabs the drumstick.

In Adrian Miller's book *Soul Food: The Surprising Story of an American Cuisine*, he explains that African American food has been called by a number of different names over the centuries "since enslaved West Africans arrived in British North America: Slave food, the master's leftovers, southern food, country cooking, home cooking, down home cooking, Negro food, and soul food. Those are the more polite names that have been used." He acknowledges that soul food suffers from an image problem, one that he considers to be generally unfair. But with its historic overreliance on animal fat, sugar, and frying, it has gained a reputation of being incredibly unhealthy. He writes, "The net effect is soul food has become a toxic cultural asset inside the [B]lack community and a cuisine stigmatized from the inside." He illustrates the point in the beginning of his book by recounting a scene in a television sitcom where a "typical middle-class African American family sits down to eat a meal together." When the grandmother is asked by her grandson what soul food is, she replies, "The number two cause of death of [B]lack men under forty."

But these are the stereotypes attached to Black people and to poor people that deserve to be challenged. We often cook soul food without the fat and the sugar. I do not recall my mother's food being greasy. Many white people of all income levels enjoy this cuisine. Once I went to a doctor, who happened to be white, and said that I wanted to lose weight. Without hesitation, her first words were, "You need to stop eating all that fried chicken."

Just let that sit for moment. I was talking to a medical professional, expressing a health concern that I wanted to address, and I was immediately assaulted by a racial stereotype. I will not begin to unpack how insulting this was—not to mention inaccurate, since I rarely indulge in fried chicken. But it also reveals the aggressive biases of others when it comes to imagining the diets of Black, brown, and poor people. I look back on my childhood and, in retrospect, I can see that our diets were healthier back then. Our meals didn't come out of cans, nor were they highly processed. Today we talk about regenerative agriculture and grass-fed meat; when we were children, those terms didn't exist, but when we ate meat, it was never fattened with chemicals. It was pure, uncontaminated, and our way of life.

What we call soul food is part of a noble and expansive gastronomic tradition. When people from West Africa were brought in shackles to North America, especially to the Southern states, they "began recreating home as best they could," Miller writes, which meant integrating foods they already knew like "chile peppers, rice, collard and turnip greens, maize, and sweet potatoes. For the New World foods they didn't know, the enslaved relied heavily on local Native Americans for guidance. From this vibrant process an identifiable cuisine took shape. Yet the freedom to shape this cuisine only went as far as what the master permitted slaves to grow, procure, cook, and eat." For me, the soul food origin story is pretty straightforward: it was the food that slave masters didn't eat, food they either ignored or discarded, and with creativity and determination, Black people turned that food into delicacies.

Parts of the pig and other animals on the plantation that were thrown away—the ears, the hocks, the tails—became rich and delectable stews (although, to be honest, this was not a part of my diet growing up). The cornmeal and flour that seemed to be abundant we turned into bread or pie crusts. My father recalled being a child and going to the market in Selma to buy bulk food. They would return with big burlap sacks of cornmeal and flour—they called them "croker" sacks—and when the sacks were emptied out, they often were repurposed into articles of clothing.

What we so often forget is that poor white people, especially in the South, had the same experience. We saw it with Toby on our drive to Auburn. For all our vast differences, in a strange way we share the same palate, because we share the same history. Southern food, country food, soul food is created to appeal to the senses—it needs to look, smell, feel, and taste good. But it also needs to connect us to each other and to our cultural traditions. All food is a form of identity, but soul food carries within it vast individual and collective histories of suffering, determination, grit, creativity, liberation, and community.

When we finish our meals, the poundcake, red velvet cake, and banana pudding demand our attention. But we need to get to Auburn. And as Toby sighs with satisfaction, he assures us he can't eat another bite. (I can't say that I completely believe him.) A large lunchtime crowd has settled in at the café in the meantime. A group of white ladies in sweater sets with expensive purses are giving their orders. At another table, two Black men, one wearing a minister's collar, are deep in conversation. A mixed-race young professional group who look like they just wandered down from the government buildings up the street are reading the menu.

Throughout the space locals and visitors are gathered because they know that what they are about to eat is something special.

After we pay, I look at the "Quote of the Week" written in chalk on a small blackboard. This one was by the writer and humorist Arnold H. Glasow. "The key to everything is Patience," it said. "You get the chicken by hatching the egg, not by smashing it."

No one contests that free or reduced-cost school meals go a long way to help students succeed socially and academically. Young people need nutrition to thrive and learn, and research bears out that reducing obesity rates, poor health, and food insecurity are all the downstream benefits for students who receive free or reduced-price school lunches. No matter where I was a teacher—whether in Washington, DC; Detroit; or North Carolina—I could see that the children who had breakfast and a good lunch would do better in school. And yet, in the last urban school where I taught, I despaired when I saw lunches that looked like a fast-food banquet: french fries, pizza, hot dogs, but few salads or vegetables. I thought to myself, What is going on? This is not food that is part of a normal diet. This should be food that is occasionally, very occasionally, offered as a treat.

When I was teaching in Washington, DC, President Ronald Reagan declared that ketchup could be considered a vegetable. It seemed a sensible strategy to his policymakers, as they were trying to slash $1.5 billion from children's nutrition programs. We didn't know whether to laugh or cry. And things have only gone downhill since then. In this country with so much wealth, children are going hungry. In 2023, South Dakota governor Kristi

Noem rejected a federal program that would have alleviated food insecurity in the state by providing $7.5 million for poor children, many of them from Indigenous families, to have lunches over the summer. (Noem said it was "too challenging to administer the program.") I know how rural communities often become food deserts—there are fewer grocery stores, and the logistics of traveling to shopping centers can sometimes be complicated. The result is a crisis in food insecurity that at least can be alleviated by meals at schools.

But the problem today, as I saw when I was still teaching, is also the kinds of meals that kids are getting. These foods are not just packed with empty calories; they are fueling a catastrophic obesity crisis in the United States, with some of the highest rates of childhood obesity on the planet. The T.H. Chan School of Public Health at Harvard University notes that in the US over the last thirty years, childhood obesity rates have tripled. Data from the 2020–2021 National Survey of Children's Health found the prevalence of obesity among American children is about 17 percent, but there is a notable regional disparity. A report from the Robert Wood Johnson Foundation showed that Utah's rate is the lowest in the country, with only 8.7 percent of the kids being obese. The farther one moves south, the farther one moves to the highest rates in the country: Mississippi tops the chart with 26.1 percent of all children and adolescents within the clinically obese category. And when the research was broken down to demographic groups, Hispanic children, non-Hispanic Black children, and non-Hispanic Indigenous children had far higher rates than other groups.

Woven throughout these grim statistics is an invisible fact: Many of the obese populations studied have experienced lives of trauma. Stress is a known contributor to inflammation and weight gain. When one considers how generational trauma exists throughout the Black, brown, and poor white communities, it is hardly surprising that obesity becomes a condition plaguing generations.

Specialists have pointed to the prevalence of processed and fast foods as contributing to this crisis. When I look back, I know that no one in my high school would ever have complained about our school lunches or viewed them as anything but healthy and nutritious. Miss Ruthie Foster, wearing her white uniform, a net over her red hair, and plastic gloves on her hands, was our dietitian and the woman who made sure that all the children—and there were a lot of them from Head Start and pre-K all the way through high school—received food cooked with care and love, from scratch, every day. The ladies who worked in the kitchen had children in school too, so formal and informal family connections were present in nearly every grade. My brother and I would reminisce about the food in high school. Can you imagine a young person in high school today doing that twenty or thirty years from now? My favorite was the spaghetti and meat sauce and the buttered rolls. When I caught the aroma of those rolls as it traveled throughout the school, I didn't just feel hunger in my stomach; I felt what I can only describe as desire. My brother still thinks fondly of banana pudding, barbeque pork, and hamburgers.

Given my line of work, I cannot help but be concerned about the effects rising temperatures will have on our food supply.

Climate change has already compromised food security. A recent study warned that more than 90 percent of fish, shellfish, plants, and algae, not to mention hundreds of species farmed in fresh water, are at risk from rising temperatures and pollution, and 2023 was officially the hottest year in the Earth's history.

I attended a conference in Chicago in 2008 sponsored by the Federation of Southern Cooperatives. During one of the sessions, a woman asked about the nutritional implications of food sourced globally versus locally. If food came from halfway around the world, what kind of preservatives were necessary to get it from a field to a supermarket thousands of miles away? What kind of nutritional deterioration takes place in transit?

I DELIVER MY LECTURE on environmental and sanitation justice at Auburn University before several hundred students and faculty members. I recount my own story, the story of my community in Lowndes County, and how poverty and sanitation are concerns shared by all races, indeed all over the world. One young white man in the audience asks lots of questions and announces himself as a conservative Republican. Later, when he comes up to have me sign a copy of my first book, he tells me that his grandparents live in a trailer in a rural Alabama community and struggle with their septic system. He asks if I can help his family. I assure him that I would be happy to. A young white woman introduces herself and mentions that her grandparents were from Lowndes County—her last name is the same as the owner of the local general store where my great-great-grandfather worked. A young Black woman tells me she has been organizing dinners for low-income students on campus whose stipends are inadequate to cover meals and housing and books. At the reception following the talk, I notice that she folds up some extra sandwiches in a napkin and puts them in her backpack.

The next day after the two classes I teach, a different driver, Serenity, appears at the hotel. She is a large young Black woman with an easy laugh and a confident manner. She immediately engages us in conversation as we pull away from the hotel. I tell her that we have one short stop to make en route, in the parking lot of a Montgomery hotel where one of my nieces is waiting with two dozen red velvet cupcakes from JoZettie's Cupcakes, created by Mrs. Ida, the best baker in the city. Her story is one that bears retelling. Mrs. Ida lived and worked in Montgomery before moving to New Orleans, where she worked for a renowned bakery. She returned to Montgomery, fell on hard times, and, "looking to God for direction," she saw a "For Rent" sign in front of a vacant building, decided to put a deposit down on the building, and opened a bakery. Merging the names of her father and mother, JoZettie's Cupcakes was born. Soon it became a local institution, famous for its cupcakes, cakes, cookies, and pies. My daughter had asked that we bring some cupcakes home, and my niece, who had recently graduated from Auburn with a journalism degree, agreed to pick them up—provided she got some too.

In 1911, a cookbook appeared entitled *Good Things to Eat, as Suggested by Rufus: A Collection of Practical Recipes for Preparing Meats, Game, Fowl, Fish, Puddings, Pastries, Etc.*, and among the 591 recipes is one for a sweet velvet cake. It was the first cookbook written by a Black chef, a man named Rufus Estes who had been born a slave. He joined the railroad and worked his way up to become a Pullman private-car attendant. In that prestigious position, he served President Grover Cleveland, President William Henry Harrison, the African explorer Sir Henry Morton Stanley, and other notables of the time. He was then hired by a man known as John "Bet-a-Million" Gates, a Chicago entrepreneur and industrialist who made his fortune by selling barbed wire and, yes, gambling. As Gates's private chef in Chicago, Rufus established himself within that community, and after Gates died, he was hired by US Steel as chef to its corporate chief. In his cookbook, Rufus included recipes for all sorts of desserts, including crullers, cranberry sherbet, maple parfait, and a sweet, but not red, "velvet cake."

Which brings me back to the red velvet cake. It turns out there is a rich and uncertain history about its origins. Some food historians suggest that brown sugar was once called "red sugar" and used in velvet-style cakes. Others point out that beet juice was used to moisten cakes during the Great Depression, when eggs and butter were rationed. In the 1930s, red food coloring first appeared, and that is when the cakes assumed their vivid color and appeared on the menus of the luxury Waldorf Astoria Hotel restaurant in New York and the Canadian department store chain Eaton's. Apparently, there is a debate among food scholars as to whether red velvet cake should be considered soul food or not, but the debate does not interest me at all.

During Juneteenth celebrations of our ancestors' emancipation from slavery, red velvet cake appears on tables all over the country. The cake's red color symbolizes so much: the blood of our enslaved ancestors, the blood spilled in the fight against slavery, and the colors of foods in West Africa, where red is thought to suggest rare mystical and spiritual powers.

After we collect the cupcakes, we get on the road north to Huntsville, and Serenity shares her family's story. Her mother was only sixteen years old when she gave birth to Serenity. Serenity had her first child at eighteen and another soon after. Today, five women and three generations live together. Serenity talks about her sixteen-year-old daughter, who was 435 pounds before her bariatric surgery and is now down to 375. She wanted her daughter to have the best surgeon in Montgomery, and by all accounts the surgery went well. But now it's Serenity's turn for the operation, and she tells us she's decided to go to Mexico for the surgery, where it's much cheaper. Her insurance won't cover Ozempic, the new but very expensive diabetes drug used for weight loss, so she doesn't feel she has much choice.

How was it that over two days and about six hundred miles, traveling back and forth from Huntsville to Auburn, the legacy of food in our community came into such sharp relief? All the joy of it—and all the ways it seems to have gone terribly out of whack. How the special fun of sharing a soul-food meal with Toby and taking a brief detour for our red-velvet-cupcake treasures is woven into the lifelong struggles of people like Serenity and her family. It seems that for them, food has almost nothing to do with the terrible weight they must endure. And yet, of course, it has everything to do with it.

We Americans have a worldwide reputation for being overweight, and as other developing countries confront their own struggles with obesity, they point to us not just as examples of the problem but as the source of their dysfunction. America's fast-food exports! America's portion-size obsession! America's highly processed foods! American exceptionalism is no longer the case, it seems, when it comes to eating habits. But perhaps we can turn to some places in Europe for guidance in coming up with solutions.

In 2005, the well-known British chef Jamie Oliver—who became famous as the "Naked Chef," a reference to the simplicity of his recipes, not his wardrobe—decided to use his fame to help change school meals in the United Kingdom. He embarked on a campaign to eliminate processed foods and replace them with healthy foods—lots of fruits, vegetables, whole grains, beans, salads, and lean meat. Foods we all know are good for us. Five years into his campaign, studies showed that the children who ate the healthy lunches also performed better on tests.

He was sure he could replicate his success in the US—or at least in a small part of it. In 2010, he visited Huntington, West Virginia, where a school breakfast consisted of an egg-and-cheese-smothered "breakfast pizza" and chocolate milk, illustrating why the community was designated by the Centers for Disease Control and Prevention as America's fast-food capital. This was a perfect spot to foment what he called a "food revolution." His efforts to replace chicken nuggets and fries with roast chicken and wild rice were not successful, and I'm not sure that he ever gained any real traction here in the way that he did in the UK. But then again, the British government robustly supported his efforts, something unlikely to happen here.

Then there is the program in Italy, where schoolchildren learn about Italian cuisine while feasting on the Mediterranean diet of fresh local foods. Once more, the government took the lead in making this program available to children all over the country. The Ministry of Health directed schools to source food locally and offered them clear guidelines for what is (organic food!

locally sourced!) and is not (processed food! junk!) acceptable. Meanwhile, children are also learning all about the food they're eating—what explains all the colors of vegetables, for instance, or how fish and meat differ nutritionally.

It wasn't so long ago that we had a government that wanted to encourage healthy eating. After all that's happened in our country in recent years, it seems as if Michelle Obama's efforts on behalf of healthier school lunches happened in another lifetime. But back in 2012, radically improved nutrition standards for school meals were implemented as a response to the 2010 Healthy, Hunger-Free Kids Act. It was all a part of Mrs. Obama's Let's Move program, which focused on diet and exercise for children in school, especially the thirty million who participated in the National School Lunch Program and the twelve million in the School Breakfast Program. For many of these children, these are the meals that stand in the way of hunger. Serenity, or one of her children, could have been in this program.

The directive was elegant in its simplicity: serve more whole grains, fruits, vegetables, and low-fat milk and dairy products; cut back on salt and fat; and reduce portion sizes. And the thing is, it worked. In 2020, researchers from the University of Washington School of Public Health found that since those changes were implemented, the overall nutritional quality of school meals markedly improved. And the study found that those children, overall, were healthier.

And then, of course, came the administration of Donald J. Trump, and everything changed. All of a sudden, white bread, chocolate milk, processed foods, and so much salt replaced the green vegetables, beans, peas, and whole grains. As usual, poor children became the victims of cruel and capricious government policies.

Still, there are some points of light outside of government programs. Kat Taylor is an activist who has led the way in a field known as regenerative agriculture—a sustainable approach to farming and food that prioritizes individual farmers all over the world. After witnessing how agribusiness ravages our environment and diets, this kind of farming holds "harm reduction" as its greatest priority—a strategy for nurturing the soil, enriching the land, and improving the cultivation and distribution of food grown by farmers. Kat and her partner, Tom Steyer, have their own ranch—TomKat Ranch in northern California—where they practice regenerative agriculture and raise grass-fed cattle on 1,800 acres. She also created a network of farmers and ranchers who share their harvest with people in need, and she supports the smaller, environmentally conscious farms and ranches owned by people of color, Indigenous people, and women.

In the nation's leading farm state, millions of lower-income California families are food insecure. When COVID ripped through the world and supply chains were disrupted, exacerbating hunger and food insecurity, Kat stepped in and created bridges between the farmers and hungry people. She went to food banks all over the state and created a supply chain between them and those who were growing and producing the food. This network delivered 138,000 pounds of fresh, organic produce to food-insecure families throughout California's Central Coast in a matter of months, and over the year, they provided nearly 850,000 pounds of fresh food throughout the state.

Kat and Tom have continued their work after the crisis of the pandemic passed, and they are enlisting the help of farmers, ranchers, scientists, and advocates to try to transform five million acres in the state into regenerative sources of food. I try to imagine what a program like this could mean in Alabama, where there is so much plenty and yet so many hungry people—many of them children. TomKat Ranch is one of the places where I find hope in this world. And when I look at Serenity and her family and all the suffering they have endured because of food, I wonder what their lives might look like had Michelle Obama, Kat Taylor, and countless other food activists been able to reach them. Perhaps they would have had access to healthier food, which would have transformed the choices they made. Given the limited options in the food desert in which they live, their fate seems predestined. But for the next generation, maybe it won't have to be. Access to healthy food should be a human right, on par with clean air to breathe and clean water to drink. As distant a possibility as this may be, I cannot feel pessimistic as I write these words. My faith sustains me in this hope, as it does in so many other parts of my life.

FOUR

The Meaning of Life

Just before Christmas in 1965, my mother was recovering from the birth of her fifth child, David, at the John A. Andrew Memorial Hospital, on the campus of the Tuskegee Institute in Alabama. She was twenty-six years old. By all measures it should have been a very happy holiday season for my parents—not just because of the arrival of the baby, but also because this was the year that the Voting Rights Act was signed into law by President Lyndon Johnson, one year after the 1964 Civil Rights Act was passed. Two momentous markers for those who had devoted so much of their lives to the Civil Rights Movement. Deep systemic racism remained, but there must have been a feeling of real hope for Black parents all over the South. Hope that their children would be safer, better educated, and have more economic and social possibilities because they would grow up in a world that was free, or maybe just freer, from the Jim Crow horrors that had scarred their lives.

And yet, while my mother was in the hospital, physicians had decided that her reproductive life should end. While she was in labor, she was told that she had to consent to tubal ligation in order for the doctor to deliver her baby. Tubal ligation, what is casually called "having your tubes tied," was part of a national program, sanctioned by state governments, that sterilized women. That the hospital was for poor women without insurance was another way that the medical establishment preyed on low-income people.

This process of forced and involuntary sterilization was referred to by activist Fannie Lou Hamer, with the mordant humor that emerges from righteous fury, as "Mississippi appendectomies." In Hamer's case, she had gone to the hospital to have a uterine tumor removed in 1961, and while she was thoroughly sedated, the doctors decided her reproductive organs should go as well. Why not? Hamer was poor and Black and likely fertile. As a Mississippi congressman had reportedly said, forced sterilization was designed to "stop this black tide which threatens to engulf us."

It is impossible to quantify how many mostly poor and mostly Black women were sterilized at the same time as my mother and Hamer. Each state had its own programs, and, even then, individual doctors could improvise with few consequences. But in 1970, during the height of the Nixon administration, when both the House and the Senate were controlled by the Democrats, Congress passed the Family Planning Services and Population Research Act. It sounds quite innocuous, doesn't it? But in fact, in what can only be described as eugenics, the act sanctioned and subsidized sterilizations of Medicaid recipients and Indian Health

Service patients. The grim numbers demonstrate its efficiency: 100,000 to 150,000 poor and mostly Black and Native women were sterilized *every year* until 1979, when federal sterilization guidelines were enacted to protect women from the procedure.

The John A. Andrew Memorial Hospital was founded in 1892 as Alabama's only hospital for Black people. It was one part of the compound created by Booker T. Washington that included a prestigious university, all designed to educate and support the Black community. In 1913, the hospital was renamed in honor of Andrew, the former governor of Massachusetts, an abolitionist who advocated for the inclusion of Black troops not just in the Union forces but in the US military. But in 1965, while my mother was in the maternity ward, in another area of the hospital, immoral experiments conducted by the US Public Health Service and the Communicable Disease Center on almost four hundred Black men who suffered from syphilis were entering their thirty-third year. The project would continue for another seven years before the practice was exposed to the press and finally ended in 1972. Not before an appalling human cost: 128 patients died of syphilis or related complications, forty wives were infected, and nineteen children were born with congenital syphilis.

But this was not yet revealed in the Christmas season of 1965.

Since 1919, Alabama had led the way among states in forcing the sterilization of people who were considered by racist and eugenicist state legislators to have demonstrated their unfitness to be a part of society. Sterilization was mandatory for people who were in hospitals, prisons, or orphanages or who were considered to be intellectually disabled, or "feebleminded," as they disparagingly said back then. The revelations from Hitler's eugenicist

Germany—which engaged in similar practices—slowed the enthusiasm in the US, but it was revived again in the 1950s, continued, and then was further supported by the government act
through the 1970s. In some teaching hospitals, poor Black women
were not told what was taking place. They were used by medical
students to perfect their technique in performing sterilizations,
much like cadavers. This was the case for my mother.

The assault on the human rights of women was federally sanctioned and federally funded through a program in which doctors
had carte blanche to sterilize women and adolescent girls and others they deemed unworthy of becoming parents. On the occasions
that they actually did inform these women of what was going to
happen, doctors quashed any protest by threatening to cut off welfare support or refusing medical services—delivering their children in a hospital, for instance. This violent act on women's bodies
gained some of its diabolical power from the secrecy surrounding
the most intimate aspects of women's lives. Yes, people knew that
it was going on, but what leverage did they have?

Finally, they found recourse in the justice system. After decades, this degrading and inhumane practice emerged from the
shadows on July 17, 1973, when the Southern Poverty Law Center
filed a lawsuit on behalf of two mentally disabled sisters, Mary
Alice and Minnie Lee Relf. Mary and Minnie were the youngest
of six children in a Montgomery family. Their parents were illiterate, and their father had been injured in an accident and unable
to work. Oh, yes, and of course they were African American. In
other words, they were perfect victims in an unjust system. The
girls were twelve and fourteen years old, and boys had begun visiting them. One day, city social workers picked the girls up, told

their mother that they were going to a family planning clinic to receive birth control shots (which, by the way, had not yet been tested on humans), and instead were taken to a hospital.

Minnie Lee, also illiterate, was the older sister and was given a consent form that she signed with an *X*. Informed consent technically granted, both girls were given tubal ligations.

Their parents were not permitted to visit them for three days. When they returned home, their father saw the scars on Minnie Lee's body. Jessie Bly, a Black social worker in the hospital, found out what had happened and told the girls' parents, which in turn led their father to demand answers. He was told they had been sterilized because they had "signed" the consent form. Bly then took the family to the Southern Poverty Law Center, which had been aware of the practice but had not yet found a suitable case to file. This one fit the bill, and the organization sued the federal government and brought the story to public attention. Senator Edward Kennedy from Massachusetts even invited the girls' parents to testify in Congress.

Between the congressional hearings and the wide publicity the Relf case received, my parents had heard of the case—as had everyone in Alabama. But for my mother, this was personal in more ways than one. At the time, she was an organizer for the National Welfare Rights Organization, a nonprofit group that fought for women and children's dignity, justice, democratic participation, and income equality. It was founded in 1966, when a group of welfare activists met and decided that a grassroots organization for poor people all across the country was necessary in order to galvanize their power within the broad framework of the Civil Rights Movement.

My mother became involved in the Alabama branch of the organization a few years later, working in the community to reach out to poor women and families to help them with their benefits and inspire them to get involved politically. In this position, when news of the Relf case broke in March 1973, she was tasked with finding and talking to women who had been sterilized, just as she had been. That part wasn't hard. Within the informal networks that existed at the time, women all over the community spoke to each other about the case and urged their sisters and friends to step forward if they too had suffered this terrible treatment.

A new dimension of my mother was revealed to me. In her quiet way, even with her sunny disposition, she carried with her the dignified but burning rage of Black women who had been grievously wronged for their entire lives. Then, when the time was right—and the story of Mary Alice and Minnie Lee made the time right—she deployed that rage for the good of others.

When my mother was sterilized, I was seven years old and of course I didn't know anything about it. After all, as the oldest child, I was a seasoned veteran of my mother being pregnant, leaving for a few days, and returning with a squalling baby. I seem to remember that it felt as if she was gone for a longer time when she gave birth to my youngest brother, but I didn't think twice about that. In 1973, when I was fifteen, the word spread about her work with the National Welfare Rights Organization. I will never fully know the backstory, but I assume that journalists were in touch with the Alabama branch of the ACLU, which was in touch with the National Welfare Rights Organization, who identified my mother as a good source for a story about the issue, as she was both a victim and an advocate.

A television reporter from Montgomery, a lawyer from the American Civil Liberties Union, a local reporter from the NBC affiliate in Montgomery, and a reporter and crew from the BBC appeared at our house in Lowndes County. My brothers were wearing their ironed white shirts, my sister and I wore nice dresses, and we all quietly watched the proceedings in our front yard as the BBC reporter interviewed my mother, who shared her story.

My parents got married a year after I was born, but their devotion had long preceded my birth. They met in Birmingham in 1957, and when my father saw young Mattie Debardelaben walking down the street, he smiled and said to his friends, "Here comes my wife." He must have been struck by her serene manner, her caring expression, and her quiet elegance. I always thought that my mother was tall—she had a bearing that made her appear to be—but in fact, she was only five feet two inches, just like me. She was dark-skinned with wide-set, heavy-lidded eyes, and when she smiled her dimples were revealed. She was a proper lady, who always wore lipstick and nail polish. And when it was time for church, my mother chose from a vivid collection of hats.

My father was about five feet nine inches and usually dressed in the gray or blue work clothes that were basically his uniform—except when he went to church, or when he was being interviewed with my mother by the BBC. They were both very community-oriented. My mother was more of the teacher, thoughtful, soft-spoken, providing guidance to young women who sought her out. Most of her jobs were as an organizer or an advocate. Her mother had died when she was fifteen years old, leaving eight motherless children behind. My mother was the youngest, and she had five siblings who lived in Detroit, a brother who lived in Birmingham, a brother in New Jersey, and her oldest sister, Eula, whom we affectionately called Aunt Honey, who stayed in the family's hometown in Autauga County.

My father was an only child, but most of the people in Lowndes County were in some way related to him. He treasured being part of a big family. That was one of the things that led to my interest in genealogy: I could not understand how someone with no siblings could have so many cousins. When I heard my father speak—many people said he had the voice and the measured, articulate style of Dr. King—he reminded me of a preacher. Folks would ask him where his church was because of his powerful, charismatic presence.

And so, as the cameras rolled and the reporter took notes, the two of them spoke about what had happened to my mother. What struck me as I listened to them were the years of pain that my mother had never shared, the suffering I had never known about, and the injustice that was never addressed. As children, we didn't really have access to the intimacy our parents shared as a couple, but during this interview, the love and care and profound mutual respect that bound them for more than four decades was undeniable. In speaking out that day, my mother was encouraging other women to tell their stories and share them publicly. Much like during the wastewater crisis many years later, people were ashamed of their circumstances, locked in their need for privacy. When she spoke that day, she referred to other women who had undergone the same experience in Tuskegee and showed the world that one didn't need to have been young or developmentally disabled or impoverished to have been violated. You could be articulate, married, and respectable and still have been victimized by a brutal system.

In 1974, the girls finally won their lawsuit, *Relf v. Weinberger* (Caspar Weinberger was the head of the Department of Health and Human Services at the time). Judge Gerhard Gesell, a judge in the powerful United States District Court for the District of Columbia, wrote in his decision, "The dividing line between family planning and eugenics is murky." He described the forced sterilizations in the 1970s as having "improperly coerced" poor women and banned the use of federal funds for any sterilization that was performed without informed consent. He also made sure that local welfare departments could no longer threaten poor women with the loss of their public assistance if they refused to submit to being sterilized. This abominable program was finally shut down in 1979 when federal guidelines outlined very clear protections, even for people who might have sought the end of their reproductive lives.

In December 2015, when these women were well past middle age, the US Senate passed a measure to address the horrors that had been inflicted, but only three states—Virginia, North Carolina, and California—created programs to compensate victims. North Carolina set up a $10 million fund for victims, though only a limited number of women were deemed eligible. Two hundred twenty women in North Carolina received about $45,000. In Virginia, the victims were given $25,000. In California, an unknown number of women, many of them Hispanic, were sterilized in the LA County General Hospital. In 2022, the state legislature created the California Forced or Involuntary Sterilized Compensation Program, and it included both an awareness campaign and funds for survivors from state hospitals or prisons. Finding the victims, however, after so much time has passed, has proven difficult.

As for the Relf sisters, they received nothing. No damages, no financial compensation. Alabama offered nothing to those who had been sterilized, and the federal government has not intervened. Minnie Lee and Mary Alice, now in their sixties, survive on their Social Security checks.

WE NEVER SAW THE BBC DOCUMENTARY. We never spoke much about what my mother had endured. Life, of course, goes on, and ten years later, in 1983, I visited friends in Chattanooga, Tennessee. I left Atlanta, where I lived at the time, to go on the trip, even though I wasn't feeling very well. Once I arrived in Chattanooga, I started experiencing extreme bouts of nausea and had a sharp pain in my right side. Alarmed, I called the physician I had been seeing in Atlanta to ask for guidance. "When you come to see me," he said dismissively, "I am going to remove your uterus because it is rotten anyway." He suggested some aspirin and went no further. His nurse overheard the conversation, called me back, and said her sister worked for a doctor in Chattanooga. She asked for my permission to put her sister in touch with me, which of course I gave. She offered a final bit of advice before hanging up: she told me never to see the Atlanta doctor again.

I was really getting concerned at this point. The pain grew more intense, and I thought that maybe the source was my appendix. I spoke to the nurse's sister, and she immediately got me an appointment with the Chattanooga physician. He had a kind bedside manner, suspected I had an infection, ordered a pregnancy test, and sent me to the hospital across the street for further tests.

A short time later, I lay on a gurney, sedated but aware of what was going on around me. I was in the hospital's operating room and faced emergency surgery. I overheard the anesthesiologist as he entered say, "I can't give her this medication—she's pregnant." There I was, in a twilight state of consciousness, and I felt a burst of excitement at the thought that I was carrying a child. Only a moment later, I learned that I could not carry this pregnancy to term. The pregnancy was irrelevant, my doctor said, because it was an ectopic pregnancy, which is to say it was a nonviable pregnancy located in a fallopian tube.

Helpless and unable to speak, I learned they were going to perform surgery to try to save the tube where the embryo had implanted. When an embryo implants in a fallopian tube, surgery is essential to prevent the tube from rupturing and creating life-threatening internal bleeding. Was this some kind of nightmarish replication of what doctors had inflicted on my mother and so many other Black women? I trusted these doctors; it was clear that they had located the cause of my discomfort. And yet, rationally and irrationally, I felt the danger of becoming another link in the long chain of victimized, experimented-on, mutilated Black women. Times have changed, I thought. It is a thing of the past. But the horrifying question was impossible to ignore: Would they sterilize me too?

That did not happen. But a quieter lack of respect did. I consented to the surgery generally but without being told that I was pregnant and that the surgery involved resectioning my tube—removing the embryo and then reconnecting the fallopian tube to

my ovary. I would have liked to have been told that I was pregnant. I would have liked to have known that they had to resection
the tube in order to save my life. At no moment did anyone say
to me, "Catherine, you are pregnant. But the pregnancy is complicated and cannot be carried to term." That would have made a
world of difference. My demeaning treatment notwithstanding,
the operation saved my life. And yet, I had always longed to be a
mother, so when I recovered from this ordeal, I grieved.

I write this after the Supreme Court *Dobbs* decision overturned
the constitutional right to an abortion and antiabortion legislatures all over the country have engaged in an orgy of restrictions
on basic health care for women. I know that had I been in exactly
the same situation in, say, Ohio or Texas or Louisiana today, the
doctors might have been unsure of what to do. Not because they
were not trained to recognize a life-threatening pregnancy gone
awry, but because if they intervened medically, they could face
criminal charges.

What had implanted in my fallopian tube was not a viable
embryo at all, but tell that to Representative John Becker from
Ohio. He authored legislation in which surgery for abortion services would be covered by health insurance only to save a woman's
life—a standard that is almost impossible to regulate—or in the
case of an ectopic pregnancy. But he had a unique approach to the
latter that had nothing to do with best practices developed over
decades. Under his plan, the physician would be required "to re-
implant the fertilized ovum into the pregnant woman's uterus."
This is medically impossible, just to be clear. And, depending on
the state, this could have happened to me—not during the Jim
Crow era, but in the twenty-first century in the richest country

on the planet. I would have been left to suffer, possibly go septic, with the threat of death before my situation would be deemed a sufficient emergency to require help.

Because of my ectopic pregnancy and the effects of the surgery, becoming pregnant without medical intervention was impossible for me. Yet I longed to be a mother, so I looked into vitro fertilization, a procedure known as IVF. My partner would have to inject hormones into my body so my egg production could be stimulated, and then some would be extracted and fertilized with my partner's sperm. Then, if successful, the embryo would be implanted in my womb. For some IVF patients, those embryos would be frozen and stored, so parents could have the potential for larger families in the future. IVF has been performed millions of times; about 2 percent of all babies in the US, or more than eight million, are the result of IVF. It was a process that seemed thankfully distant from the hideous abortion wars.

Until the Alabama supreme court made sure it wasn't.

When some frozen embryos in a reproductive-medicine clinic in Mobile were mistakenly destroyed, the couples insisted that these were not mere embryos but actual children and sued the hospital under a state law, the Wrongful Death of a Minor Act. On February 16, 2024, the court ruled, in an 8–1 decision, that the embryos were minors and, as Justice Tom Parker wrote in his concurring opinion, "Human life cannot be wrongfully destroyed without incurring the wrath of a holy God." The majority opinion asserted that there was no "unwritten exception to that rule for unborn children who are not physically located 'in utero'—that is inside a biological uterus—at the time they are killed."

This ruling seemed to panic even conservative lawmakers, and our Republican-dominated state legislature immediately passed a law that offered "civil and criminal immunity for death or damage to an embryo to any individual or entity when providing or receiving goods or services related to in vitro fertilization," including retroactively.

Indeed, it appears that the court this time had gone too far, and it is heartening to see the enraged response. But this is a costly procedure, with a single IVF cycle running about $23,000; many patients require more than one cycle. FertilityIQ, an information service, notes that the average patient will spend close to $50,000 in treatment, much of which is not covered by insurance. I am happy about the outrage. Relieved to see the pushback. But I am acutely aware that when middle-class and wealthy women's bodies are the issue, the constituency representing them is robust. For poor women, not so much.

The assaults on the autonomy of poor women's bodies seem unrelenting. We like to comfort ourselves that the notion of involuntary, forced sterilization was a relic of a morally reprehensible bygone era. And yet, maybe not. On September 14, 2020, in a footnote to President Donald Trump's unconscionable treatment of migrants, a nurse named Dawn Wooten, who worked at the Irwin County Detention Center in Ocilla, Georgia, filed a whistleblower complaint. She said that Dr. Mahendra Amin—the center's leading doctor who was not even a gynecologist—allegedly told nearly every woman who went to see him that she had to have a hysterectomy. Wooten referred to him as a "uterus collector."

Adding to this atrocity, Dr. Amin spoke no Spanish, and many of the vulnerable, detained women he violated spoke no English.

The *New York Times* reported, "Both the reviewing doctors and all of the women interviewed by the *Times* raised concerns about whether Dr. Amin had adequately explained the procedures he performed or provided his patients with less invasive alternatives. Spanish-speaking women said a nurse who spoke Spanish was only sporadically present during their exams." They did not have the faintest idea what he was doing to them. Meanwhile, as an independent physician who was under contract with US Immigration and Customs Enforcement, this doctor was paid for each individual procedure that he executed.

Upon hearing about the whistleblower's complaint, House Speaker Nancy Pelosi described the conditions at the detention center as "a staggering abuse of human rights." On October 2, 2020, the House of Representatives condemned the practice in a congressional resolution. A congressional investigation finally revealed that "female detainees appear to have undergone excessive, invasive, and often unnecessary gynecological procedures" by a physician who was not even certified as a gynecologist.

And so, over these many years, Black and Indigenous women, migrant women and white women, barely adolescent girls and older women have all had the agency of their bodies seized by others with the explicit goal of controlling their reproductive lives. I think of enslaved women—my great-great-grandmothers, their sisters and friends, and other enslaved women whose bodies were trafficked and raped on the plantations of my home state. Whose children were seized and sold like animals. Whose capacity to bear children was considered either an asset or a liability but rarely something deeply personal, something that demanded autonomy.

I look at detainees whose children were ripped from them, some of whose wombs were ripped out of their bodies. Yes, I know that we have made great progress since the time when plantations dominated our economy. And yet, as we see too often with our justice system, with our economic system, with our political system, and with our medical system, the plantation mentality endures.

FIVE

Migrations, Forced and Free

For most of my six decades on this planet, I walked through the world certain of my identity as a Black woman—specifically a Black woman from the South. Even more precise, a Black woman, the descendent of enslaved people, from Lowndes County, Alabama. As far as I was concerned, there was no question that my lineage was 100 percent African. And yet, throughout my life, brief exchanges may not have shaken my certainty but intimated that perhaps my identity was not quite as straightforward as I had long believed. These incidents didn't seem freighted with importance at the time. Only in retrospect did they come together, like random puzzle pieces that suddenly snapped into place.

My mother, Mattie Coleman, described her grandmother as an Indigenous woman, or, in her words, "an Indian." As a young child this didn't seem to me to be that much of a revelation. At

Lowndes County Training School, my physical education teacher, Mrs. Lowe, would say that I looked like I had "Indian" in me. I didn't know what she meant, since back then my only frame of reference were the "Indians" on television shows of the late 1960s and early 1970s—shows like *Gunsmoke* or *Bonanza*, where, as I recall, Indigenous people were depicted in the most stereotypical ways (ways that matched what we were taught in school). Still, Mrs. Lowe would point to my high cheekbones and the shape of my eyes, convinced that her instincts were correct. And yet, Mrs. Lowe, who was a Black woman, looked very white.

Some distant connection to Indigenous people wasn't the only aspect of my life that seemed to set me apart. When I was around twenty-one years old, I lived in Los Angeles and worked at Sears in customer service. There, I met a Nigerian man known as Sugar Bear, who played for a semipro football team in West Los Angeles. "You look like a Nigerian girl just pretending to be an American" was one of the first things he ever said to me. "I can assure you I've never been to Nigeria," I told him. "I'm from Alabama!" This wasn't some random pickup line he deployed. In fact, it turned out that he was right. He recognized something that was characteristic of Nigerian women in my features; my Nigerian background was later verified by a DNA test.

There were many instances of my being mistaken for another nationality in the international city of Washington, DC. People speaking languages that I couldn't understand would approach me because they assumed that, like them, I too was a recent immigrant. I would explain that I was just (just!) an American. Apologies would follow, but so would a bit of skepticism. They were so sure I was from the place they called home.

But these were just random occurrences. My identity was fully formed by being a Black woman in the United States and all the demands, injustices, outrages, community, and racism, explicit and implicit, that came with it. I was the oldest child of Mattie and J. C. Coleman. Indeed, that identity was more than enough.

My parents were civil rights activists who lived in Montgomery and Birmingham before moving to Lowndes County—where my father was from—to raise me, my sister, and my three brothers in a more rural community. My father was very interested in the pan-African movement, which was gaining traction at the time. We embraced this identity and would call ourselves African American and wear natural hair. My father often would say that we were of African origin, but his mother would have none of it. "We are not from Africa!" she would say with some exasperation. "I don't know why he's telling you that!" At the time, this may have been an example of the generation gap between a group of elders who prided themselves on their propriety and young people chafing and eager to express new and radical identities. We children absorbed it all but never really doubted who we were or where we came from. Those of blessed memory rested peacefully in the local cemetery. I only needed to go there, or to my mother's family's community in Autauga, and my genealogy was laid out before me.

Fifty years later, when DNA tests became readily available, I became curious about my ancestry and, like millions of others, spit into a small vial before sending my sample off to a company, this one in Canada, for the secrets of my distant past to be revealed. The testing organization presented the results in a written analysis. They also included a list of living relatives—people who also had taken that particular test—and where they were located around the world. I was very surprised. My ancestors did not just appear in Africa and Alabama; they were all over the globe. I had one relative in Somalia; I had relatives in Western and Eastern Europe; I had lots of relatives in the Caribbean, especially in Cuba and Jamaica. I had another relative in Nova Scotia.

Sugar Bear, the Nigerian in LA, was on to something since my Nigerian ancestry was revealed in a second DNA test I took with another company. But unlike most of my African ancestry, the Nigerian evidence was relatively recent—first appearing in the nineteenth century, whereas my connection to African hunter-gatherers and a presence in North Africa dated back to the sixteenth century. Tendrils of my DNA, in the eighteenth and nineteenth centuries, could be found in France, Germany, Great Britain, Portugal, Angola, and the Congo. Moving farther east, my ancestors appeared in China, Thailand, even Vietnam. They could have been farmers or aristocrats, matriarchs or healers. They could have been all these things and more. Quite literally the whole world unfolded before me. When I discovered my French lineage, I understood in a new way the uncanny sense of familiarity and ease I felt the first time I visited Paris.

The sequencing of DNA did not only offer remarkable new opportunities for curing diseases, anticipating health outcomes, cloning vegetables, or accessing traces of our lineage; it also proved once and for all that race is a social construct. When scientists initially managed to figure out the first complete genome, they used samples from a variety of people who self-identified as being from many different races. What they found was explained simply by Dr. Craig Venter, a biotechnologist who led the group of scientists in sequencing the human genome. He announced the findings of the Human Genome Project at the White House in 2000. "The concept of race," he said, "has no genetic or scientific basis."

The origins of the human species go back hundreds of thousands of years. Over many millennia, starting about sixty thousand years ago, just a few thousand people traveled from the African continent and resettled, ultimately, all over the world. They encountered humans; the Neanderthals, who appeared from the North; and a group known as the Denisovans, who emerged from the East. From these migrations, new generations were born and thrived and, in turn, also migrated. David Reich, a Harvard paleogeneticist, told *National Geographic* that in some populations, genetic differences have been rendered nearly irrelevant because of migration. "What the genetics shows is that mixture and displacement have happened again and again and that our pictures of past 'racial structures' are almost always wrong."

The way society is organized, however, defies, often violently, those scientific truths. Our institutions, our social structures, our ways of looking at the world, and our religious preferences underscore the reality of racial divides. It is the great paradox of our world: scientifically, race is insignificant and not a valid concept. And yet, it is inescapable and often is a variable that determines the difference between life and death. Even when it is not, it becomes a significant point of definition—individually, economically, socially, religiously, politically—by practically every imaginable metric.

For me, though, my DNA discovery made me realize that my ancestors were far more mobile than I had known, and that my origin story is much more complicated and nuanced. Our history as Black Americans is a lot deeper and broader than we had imagined. Before taking that DNA test, I would often hear that it was impossible to trace our lineage further back, beyond slavery. Our history, we were led to believe, started with slavery—perhaps in 1619, when the first enslaved people were brought to this country. Now, I can trace my ancestry to an African hunter-gatherer about eight generations before me. But I also see Spanish and Portuguese connections around that time. What did all these algorithms suggest about identity? Did learning this change my sense of self?

IN WAYS BOTH SUBTLE AND PROFOUND, my relationship to my work as a climate activist was transformed by my DNA revelation. Initially, my center of gravity had been Lowndes County, Alabama. My work on the sewage crisis in poor rural communities began in my own backyard, and I was determined to elevate the cause of sanitation rights to the level of inalienable human rights. In doing so, I ventured far beyond the American South, to other cities, other states, other countries. Even though I was not a conventional tourist, and even though I developed strong relationships with both activists and citizens in these places, a part of me always felt a sense of belonging, almost like déjà vu.

Now I understood why. My DNA test revealed how deeply interconnected and global our roots are, and as we share roots, so too do we share the consequences of a warming planet and the environmental devastation that we have wrought. Those longitudinal, multigenerational essences that determine who we are mirror, across the same span of time, the terrible violence that has been exacted by the climate and the environment. The extreme weather, the rising seas, the fires and terrible heat—they may appear in particular spots on the globe, but none can be siloed off by country or continent, by class or privilege, or, yes, by race or ethnicity. As far as climate was concerned, to turn the cliché on its head, one could not think only locally; one had to think globally. Climate change is occurring always, everywhere, all at once. Our carbon footprint does not have boundaries. Rising seas do not respect national interests. Inadequate infrastructure will compromise every part of a community. Smoke in Alberta, Canada, will turn the sky of North Alabama, thousands of miles away, orange. The urgency of my work became even more informed by the feeling of being connected. Connected like a family—with concern and love and considerable worry about the future our children and grandchildren will face.

Once you begin the DNA journey, it leads to unexpected people entering your life. When I was in Paris for the UN Climate Change Conference in 2015, I received an email from a woman from Nova Scotia who told me that I was connected to her husband. She wrote: "I plugged in our matching segment to Genome Mate, which helps me keep track. You are overlapping on a Nova Scotia 'pile up' segment. Because of the others' known ancestry, it's likely you're descended from one of Philippe Mius d'Entremont's sons. If you have many matches with the names Muise, Meuse, Mius, Muis, etc. and have a sliver of Native American (you do! just checked), you are likely from the son Philippe Mius D'Azy, who married two different Mi'kmaq women. Many of those families fled to Louisiana (Acadians/Cajuns). Some returned to Nova Scotia years later and some stayed in the south. So just a heads-up on that line, it's an interesting read if you google Philippe Mius d'Entremont."

The timing was serendipitous. The United Nations Climate Change Conference, known as COP, is attended by representatives from all over the world—the European Union and, back then, 195 nations, all charged with negotiating a global agreement to reduce greenhouse gas emissions. It was my first time in Europe, and I was representing the Center for Earth Ethics, a project run by former vice president Al Gore's daughter Karenna that focuses on the vast moral implications of our relationship with, in their words, "the planet as a living whole."

When I started researching the names that the woman from Nova Scotia had sent me, I learned that her husband and I were both descended from two sixteenth-century fur trappers from France, the d'Entremonts, who had received a grant of land from the French royals for a region that once was called Acadie and is now Nova Scotia. They became a notable family in both Canadian and French history. These trappers married Indigenous women, and about a hundred years later their descendants moved to Louisiana and became the original Cajuns. I was very familiar with Louisiana, because this too was a place suffering from shocking examples of environmental injustice. I had visited Revere, Louisiana, in 2019, where a petrochemical plant is located next to an elementary school.

This may have been my first trip to Paris, but from the moment I boarded the Air France flight, I had a strange sense of comfort and familiarity. The food, naturally, was divine, but more than that, I felt as if it always had been a part of my diet. The language, which I do not speak, felt oddly accessible—indeed, one of my brothers is a great Francophile. I've always been drawn to the art, especially the Impressionists, so I was eager to visit the Musée D'Orsay.

Just days before I left for Paris, a terrible, coordinated terrorist attack had taken place in the city, killing 130 people and wounding 600 others. ISIS took credit for the attack. Explosions rocked a crowded stadium during a soccer match, and another bomb went off outside the stadium. Multiple gunmen with assault weapons opened fire at a busy intersection, at several restaurants, and in a concert hall. A suicide bomber blew himself up inside another restaurant. The scenes from Paris streets, blocked off with police and ambulances, played out endlessly on CNN and other stations. I was devastated, and yet I was not afraid. I felt protected by my mission and by an opportunity I could never have imagined was possible.

After we landed at Charles de Gaulle, I took a taxi to a small school outside the city, where I met with young climate activists—many from HBCUs in the US. So yes, a bit of home appeared in Paris. But as I walked through the city, ate the food, and observed the Parisians, I didn't feel like a stranger.

All these impressions and connections oddly made the email I received from Nova Scotia feel less surprising, almost inevitable. I had never been to Nova Scotia but had always associated it with a pristine seaside landscape, so I got curious about what was happening there environmentally. I found a report from the Department of Environment and Climate Change in Nova Scotia and saw that it faced a dire future. The report warned that the province was in danger of rising temperatures, less snow, and more intense rain, with frequent and violent storms. Nova Scotia is surrounded by water, and the sea level will continue to rise. In the 2030s, flooding will pose the greatest danger, while only twenty years later warmer temperatures will make wildfires the greatest threat and diminish the region's ability to produce food.

Once more the world was made smaller by the community of suffering from climate change. In the summer of 2023, temperatures soared across France, reaching 104 degrees Fahrenheit, not just for a day but for weeks. Throughout Europe, intense heat was creating misery, with inadequate air conditioning, no infrastructure to support the high temperatures, and the inevitable public health crisis. The British medical journal *The Lancet* warned that of all the capitals in Europe facing extreme heat, Paris was the most vulnerable and its population faced the highest risk of heat-related deaths. One reason was the "urban heat island effect," a phenomenon I have seen in Birmingham and Montgomery, Detroit and LA, Tucson and Las Vegas, and cities all over the world. All the buildings, cars, and concrete absorb a tremendous amount of heat, creating suffocating conditions. And once more, throughout the world, if someone is poor, or an infant, or a child, or elderly, no matter where they live, they will be more vulnerable than others.

France and Nova Scotia were obviously not unique in suffering the effects of our climate crisis. Climate change is global and simultaneous and local. In 2022, months of catastrophic rainfall from the summer through the early fall impacted Nigeria, Chad, Niger, and surrounding countries—all of which were homes to my people—killing more than 1,500 and displacing approximately 3.2 million more. And Niger, Nigeria, and Senegal are projected to have some of the highest climate-migration numbers in the world by the end of this century.

Where will all these climate refugees go? There already is a global refugee crisis, with huge numbers of people displaced by conflict and climate and oppression. I mentioned that seeing my DNA clearly showed me that my ancestors were far more mobile than I had previously imagined, and yet mobility is an ambiguous concept. Was their migration forced or free? Some of my ancestors were shackled, transported in the boats of those who trafficked human beings. And apparently some of my Portuguese and Spanish ancestors may have been working on the boats as traffickers. My other ancestors who went to Canada from France moved with the hope of greater economic opportunity. Every migration is complex and nuanced.

Even before our tumultuous times, drought drove some who were settled and tending crops away from their homes. The hunter-gatherers moved with their prey. Now, as the climate changes, as five-hundred-year storms seem to be occurring every few years, even months, people like those 3.2 million Africans are robbed of any choice. While some parts of Africa were deluged in 2022, in West Africa—yes, I have ancestors there—the heat was nearly unbearable. Temperatures in that region have increased by one to three degrees Celsius since the mid-1970s, and while that may seem negligible, the reality is dire. Extreme heat has withered crops and forced otherwise self-sufficient communities into exile or starvation. Repeatedly we hear that warming temperatures and more frequent excessive heat and rain have created cycles of drought and flood with ruinous effects on individuals and communities. With food and water insecurity, people have lost livelihoods, they compete for limited resources, and political and social instability are inevitable.

The implications for public health are grave. When I worked on the sanitation crisis in Lowndes County, I contacted Dr. Peter Hotez, an infectious disease specialist at the National School of Tropical Medicine at Baylor College of Medicine. Together, we conducted a study of people living in Lowndes County to see how they fared in terms of disease. It took three years, but the findings were explosive. As *The Guardian* reported, "Children playing feet away from open pools of raw sewage; drinking water pumped beside cracked pipes of untreated waste; human feces flushed back into kitchen sinks and bathtubs whenever the rains come; people testing positive for hookworm, an intestinal parasite that thrives on extreme poverty. These are the findings of a new study into endemic tropical diseases, not in places usually associated with them in the developing world of sub-Saharan Africa and Asia, but in a corner of the richest nation on Earth: Alabama."

The article went on to describe my work and the conditions of my home county—the poverty, with the average annual income at the time only $18,046; the pervasive raw sewage; and the return of illnesses and diseases that should have been eradicated decades earlier. Once again, what was happening there was a microcosm of what has been happening throughout the world as a result of injustice, neglect, and indifference to human impacts on the environment. Heat-related deaths in West Africa are projected to be up to nine times higher than in the period from 1950 to 2005. Infants and young children are suffering from a drastic increase in malnutrition, so their growth and cognitive development are stunted. A catastrophe that occurs in one place is implicated in the catastrophe that occurs in another.

The paradox—if it is a paradox or just another example of how injustice is exacerbated as the world warms—is that places like West Africa that contribute the least to the climate crisis suffer the most. Right before Thanksgiving 2023, Oxfam reported that "the richest one percent of the world population produced as much carbon pollution in 2019 than the five billion people who made up the poorest two-thirds of humanity." That means that seventy-seven million people were responsible for 16 percent of emissions, and the richest 10 percent accounted for half of the emissions. One of the findings that struck me like a physical blow was that it would take about 1,500 years for someone in the bottom 99 percent of the economy to produce as much carbon as billionaires do—*in one year*. As Pope Francis wrote in his encyclical on the environment, *On Care for Our Common Home*, "The gravest effects of all attacks on the environment are suffered by the poorest." The stark reality of those statistics points to yet another dire question facing humanity: How is it possible to take a global view of climate change in a way that incorporates the vast differences in power, resources, and wealth among all these countries on the planet?

It is simple to suggest that the rich countries should carry the burden for the poor ones. But the barriers to doing this are enormous, and time is of the essence. Al Gore is one of the most influential climate activists in the world, and I have had the privilege of working with him and learning from him over the years. In 2018, he spoke at a Peace and Justice Summit focusing on the environment sponsored by the Equal Justice Initiative in Montgomery,

Alabama, where I worked at the time. I interviewed him after his remarks, and one of the things he said has stayed with me. He quoted one of his favorite poets, Wallace Stevens, who was also a businessman: "After the final no, there comes a yes, and on that yes the future world depends."

"Every great morally based movement that has improved the condition of humanity has met with an endless series of noes," Gore said, invoking the great civil rights leaders of history who faced constant resistance until, through legislation or a Supreme Court decision or an unexpected election, they encountered a yes. Then, Gore continued, "They moved to the next yes. Well, the climate movement is on the cusp of that kind of change. . . . If anyone doubts that we have the will to change, just remember that the will to change is a renewable resource."

I HAVE ALWAYS BEEN a student of history. My DNA test was a different form of tracing my personal history, another way of looking back and trying to make sense of things. As it turns out, there is not a day that goes by that I don't find my perception of events in the world deepened by the sense of my genetic connection to these places.

So yes, our vast interconnectedness, our fundamental human solidarity, simply must inform our politics, our policies, and our work in addressing the multiple crises we face. Empathy and imagination go a long way toward easing resistance to change. Yet looking back is not what propels me. It certainly provides essential context, but my passion—and I think the passion of so many activists with whom I work—is propelled by my daughter and my grandchildren. Thinking about our children forces us to think about their future. My granddaughter is an infant now; her older brother is in second grade. A friend of mine once said that grandchildren are the only experience in life that is not overrated, and I have to agree with her.

I have traveled hundreds of thousands of miles, and sometimes my daughter expresses concern. "The world has become such a dangerous place," she says. "Do you really need to take this trip to the Middle East when there is a war going on?" I try to reassure her with the words that I used when she was her son's age, when there was some great tragedy in second grade. "You have to focus on something good," I tell her. "That's the way you will get to the other side because otherwise we will never do anything."

But then I also share the most important reason for why I do what I do: I want to make sure that she has a future. That my grandchildren will have a future. I want to make sure that someday, say, in the year 2225, when my great-great-great-great-grandchildren begin to explore their DNA, they may see my little blip on the map of the world. And their presence on this fragile Earth of ours in that unimaginable year will mean that this hard fight was won.

And like Wallace Stevens said, it was won because, along with so very many others, I said yes.

SIX

My Moon Shot

ON JULY 20, 1969, ALL OVER THE WORLD, PEOPLE SAT IN front of their television sets and watched a human being set foot on the moon's surface for the first time. My family was no exception. We watched, riveted, as Neil Armstrong took those first steps, followed by Buzz Aldrin. For two hours they wandered around on the brightest object in our night sky, a point of reference for our planet since before recorded time. They took photographs and harvested dust and rocks to bring back home. As a young girl, I was endlessly fascinated by space travel, astronauts, and the vast mysteries of galaxies far beyond our fragile planet. Watching men land on the moon inspired me to believe that space exploration would be a part of my future. What did it take to have the kind of imagination that could make dreams of space flight a reality?

It felt like a moment when the whole country came together, at a time when it felt like everything was coming apart. Just one year earlier, Dr. Martin Luther King Jr. had been assassinated and Rev. Ralph Abernathy, one of his closest allies, had stepped in as the leader of the Southern Christian Leadership Conference (SCLC). The right to vote and desegregation had become more widespread in the South, but battles for economic justice and security were the next crucial fronts in the war for equality.

Before his death, Dr. King had been planning another Poor People's Campaign march, as an effort to find the "middle ground between riots on the one hand and timid supplications for justice on the other." The march, tens of thousands of people strong, took place without him in Washington, DC, in August 1968, with Reverend Abernathy at the fore. An earlier event was led by King's widow, Coretta Scott King, who organized a march of women on Mother's Day 1968. The next day, a temporary settlement of tents and shacks—reminiscent of the tent city that was established on the Selma to Montgomery Trail—sprang up on the National Mall and was christened Resurrection City.

Protesters lived there for more than a month and used it as their home base before visiting federal agencies and congressional representatives to lobby for an end to poverty and an Economic Bill of Rights. Their success was modest: funds for free and reduced lunches were allocated after the demonstrations and much-needed Head Start programs were established in Mississippi and Alabama. A protest caravan was also created, in which a wagon drawn by mules made its way to the Republican National Convention in Miami Beach, Florida, and to the chaotic Democratic National Convention in Chicago.

Those mules and the wagons would make another appearance the following year.

Witnessing the buildup of the space program and the planned moon launch over the next few months, Reverend Abernathy decided to confront NASA leadership over the colossal amounts of money this project consumed. He could not fathom why those funds, creative minds, and national determination were not directed toward addressing catastrophic inequality and poverty in the nation. So he set off to bring attention to this matter in a place where he knew the public attention was already going to be focused.

On the evening of July 14, 1969—less than a week before the first moon landing—about five hundred marchers arrived at NASA's gates in Florida.

They were mostly Black men, women, and children, accompanied by those mule-drawn wagons, a way of emphasizing that for most of the world, the high-tech age of rockets bore little resemblance to the modest realities of their daily lives. Protesters held signs that read, "$12 a day to feed an astronaut, we could feed a child for $8." NASA administrator Thomas Paine met the group the next day, and Reverend Abernathy told him that he had three requests: he asked that ten families in the entourage be permitted to view the launch; that NASA "support the movement to combat the nation's poverty, hunger, and other social problems"; and that the scientists at NASA focus their work "to tackle the problem of hunger."

Today, more than fifty-five years later, I see Reverend Abernathy's list of requests as being especially prescient. Not only did he prioritize the problems he knew were inconsistent with the good of the country; he could see that NASA was a seat of innovation whose mission might go beyond the exploration of outer space. In response, Paine said, "If we could solve the problems of poverty in the United States by not pushing the button to launch men to the moon tomorrow, then we would not push that button." Paine added that he hoped Reverend Abernathy would "hitch his wagons to our rocket, using the space program as a spur to the nation to tackle problems boldly in other areas, and using NASA's space successes as a yardstick by which progress in other areas should be measured"—noting that NASA's technical advances were "child's play" compared to "the tremendously difficult human problems" Reverend Abernathy and the SCLC were managing.

Paine was able to satisfy one of the minister's more concrete demands: he gave VIP viewing-area tickets to his group so they could watch the moon shot on the following day. In exchange, he asked Reverend Abernathy to pray for the safety of the astronauts. And despite the glaring problems in the country, despite his traumatic experiences while fighting for fundamental civil rights, Reverend Abernathy expressed what my family and many Black people all over the nation felt that day: he was as proud as anyone could be at our nation's accomplishment.

Sometimes I imagine what it would have been like to have been able to seize a galvanizing historic moment, like the moon launch, the way that Rev. Ralph Abernathy did. Not just to make a bigger point about values, but to challenge a whole part of government to come up with concrete solutions and prioritize a social issue they never considered to be part of their remit. Who would have imagined that NASA could deploy its considerable resources to solve problems in the terrestrial world, like poverty and racial injustice? Or climate change and environmental justice?

Several years ago, I moved from Montgomery to Huntsville in order to live in a city with the infrastructure for innovation. Infrastructure is more than upgraded sewer systems, sound electric grids, and reliable water supplies; there is also the kind of infrastructure necessary for creativity and development: education, diversity, a robust commitment to attracting investment, and physical space to accommodate new businesses, labs, and incubators for technology. Huntsville has that.

More than three hundred companies and twenty-six thousand employees are located at Cummings, the second-largest research park in the entire country. The Redstone Arsenal, a historic US Army base, is where fifty thousand people work as employees of the Department of Justice, the Department of Defense, the FBI, and the Marshall Space Flight Center. As the rising tide lifts all boats, so too could my organization, the Center for Rural Enterprise and Environmental Justice (CREEJ), benefit from being adjacent to so many resources essential for sustainable economic growth.

But it works both ways. Having an organization committed to environmental justice located in this community, I hoped, could raise the consciousness of scientists, entrepreneurs, and tech visionaries about issues that would inspire them to expand their mandate for innovation—a moral mandate, as it were, in just the way that Reverend Abernathy had envisioned more than half a century earlier.

It makes me smile to think that NASA and I were born in the same year. In 1958, President Dwight D. Eisenhower created NASA by signing the National Aeronautics and Space Act, which defined the space program not only as a tool of national defense but also as one for scientific research and the exploration of space for peaceful purposes. Eisenhower named NASA's space flight center after General George C. Marshall in 1959, on the property of the army rocket development complex at the Redstone Arsenal in Huntsville.

When I was first traveling around Huntsville, I was struck by how many streets have German names—and the fact that there's an Oktoberfest celebration at the local military base, a biergarten at the US Space & Rocket Center on most Thursdays, and a neighborhood once dubbed "Sauerkraut Hill" by locals. I learned that right after World War II, more than 1,600 German scientists— all Nazi sympathizers and all participants in the war machine— were secreted out of their defeated country and brought to the United States. They weren't transported as the war criminals many of them were but as scientific assets. In what became known as Operation Paperclip, these engineers, physicists, and highly skilled technicians were able to shed their Nazi pasts and receive secret government jobs in the United States. A group of more than a hundred of them were moved to Redstone Arsenal in Huntsville in 1950. Their assignment was to develop new missile technology for Cold War defenses and turn the impossible vision of a man on the moon into reality.

The key to all this was the missiles, which played a critical role in the escalating Cold War between the former allies, the US and the Soviet Union. The leader of this group, the most valuable asset of all, was a former member of the Nazi Party and the SS, an aerospace engineer named Wernher von Braun. No doubt, he was a genius as a space visionary, obsessed with the idea of exploring that previously inaccessible realm from the time he was a child. Even in the early 1930s, he envisioned a highly concentrated liquid fuel that would be capable of sending a rocket into space. He was brought into the Nazi war machine to design the most efficient missiles imaginable for the Reich. He soon became the head of a rocket facility that produced the deadly V-2 rockets.

The rockets were built in a top-secret construction facility known as Mittelwerk, located near the Mittelbau-Dora concentration camp. Mittelwerk had to be nearly invisible, so most of it was located underground, a warren of damp, dark, cold tunnels. More than sixty thousand prisoners—of course, mostly Jews—were forced to work here, with more than a third dying from the punishing demands, torture at the hands of the guards, starvation, or disease. Those who stepped out of line were hung in public executions—often in groups. Here was yet another example of racist violence, of hate crimes on a massive scale on a continent far away from the one where my Black ancestors had experienced similar degradation. This was slavery, pure and simple, but this time in twentieth-century Europe. The backbreaking unpaid labor, the sadistic masters, the murder for perceived insubordination—it all sounds very familiar to Black people. But Nazi Germany instituted an additional element: crematoriums were constructed to dispense with the immense number of dead bodies.

Von Braun was not the commandant of the camp—he was said to have visited only rarely, mostly when it was under construction—but he was a part of the Nazi war machine. The missile he invented was responsible for devastation in the relentless air assaults on Antwerp, Liège, Brussels, Paris, and London during the Blitz, where these missiles rained down on civilians.

In March 1944, von Braun had gotten drunk at a party and said that he did not see how Germany could win the war. That was not his top concern, however; he wanted to keep working on his rockets, so he sought a way to engage the Americans. To me, this anecdote illustrates his cold-blooded opportunism. His loyalties clearly were malleable, but his ambition was single-minded. A few weeks later he was placed under house arrest for this transgression, though he was never sent to prison. His contribution to the Nazi war effort was just too valuable.

The following year, on May 1, 1945, while in hiding with other scientists and engineers in Bavaria, he learned that Hitler was dead. He promptly surrendered to American soldiers, along with his brother. He and hundreds of others in this elite group were given safe passage to the United States, rehabilitated without much fuss, and offered military funding to keep working on rockets. Better he and all his technological brilliance end up in America, the reasoning went, than have the Russians obtain this asset.

When the Germans and the army's missile program arrived in Huntsville in 1950, the professional opportunities appeared to be vast—if you happened to be a white man with an engineering degree. Only 16,437 people lived in the city at the time. Huntsville was just another Southern cotton-market town. For the approximately five thousand Black people who lived there, the arrival of these Germans and the flood of generous government funding at first did little to change the segregated status quo. But here's where the narrative gets especially interesting.

Local African American leaders watched the transformation of their city—the population more than quadrupled to seventy-two thousand in just ten years—and were convinced that all the new forces that were coming into play might present a unique opportunity to end segregation. In 1962, a group of these leaders created the Community Service Committee—or what they informally referred to as the "psychological warfare committee"—with the integration of the downtown Woolworth's lunch counter as a first step in the long process of breaking the grip of white supremacist leaders in the city. Nashville had accomplished this in 1960, after months of violence and protest, and throughout the South similar efforts were taking place.

Every day, as if it were a full-time job, Black men, women, and children went downtown to sit at a lunch counter. Hundreds of demonstrators participated and were arrested, but unlike similar protests throughout the South, the ones in Huntsville were relatively nonviolent. Thus, they also failed to attract much national attention, which was essential if real change was to occur.

In March 1962, the local leaders invited Dr. King to Huntsville to speak at what was then Oakwood College (today it's Oakwood University) and the First Missionary Baptist Church. The events were standing room only, and unlike many such gatherings, there were many white faces in the crowd as well. The following month, two new, sympathetic figures appeared at the local lunch counter: Martha Hereford, a very pregnant doctor's wife, and Joan Cashin, a dentist's wife who was holding her four-month-old baby—two women from middle-class professional families. Their arrests would mark a new low in the abuse of civil rights workers and draw attention to what was happening in Huntsville.

The committee understood that they were playing the long game, and the influx of government funds, new economic development, and a vastly expanded professional class had given them a different kind of economic leverage to break the chains of segregation in their city. Using the momentum from the lunch counter arrests, protesters went to Wall Street in New York City, where they passed out flyers at the Stock Exchange, exposing traders who had invested in the contractors who did business with NASA in Huntsville and urging divestment. The demonstrators shared the flyers they distributed in New York with the white city leaders back home. The implicit question was stark: What would happen to all the ambitious plans and all federal funding if investors got cold feet and private sector money started drying up?

This caught the nation's attention.

The desegregation of Huntsville's lunch counters began in July 1962. Then came integrating movie theaters and Sonnie Hereford IV's momentous appearance in the first grade of Fifth Avenue Elementary School. (The city now has a school named after him.) All public accommodations in Huntsville were desegregated two years before the 1964 Civil Rights Act was signed, and with no violence.

When people think about civil rights in Alabama, they think about Lowndes County, Selma, Montgomery, and Birmingham. They should also think about Huntsville. Because Dr. John Cashin, the Huntsville dentist whose wife was arrested, was also one of the founders of the National Democratic Party of Alabama. This party facilitated the election of more than one hundred Black people to public office in Alabama from 1968 to 1974. And Huntsville provided an opportunity for African Americans to work in the space industry with fewer restrictions than other cities in the South.

Life in the South seemed to have somehow changed von Braun. His story reminds me of the ones of old, impassioned Confederates—such as General James Longstreet, a notable wartime leader—who became advocates for Reconstruction. As Steven Moss and Richard Paul write in their introduction to the PBS series about the space race, *Chasing the Moon*, "Von Braun's public conversion was now complete. His V-2 missiles which rained death on London gave birth to the Saturn V, which propelled men to the moon. Within twenty years he had evolved from potential war criminal and refugee to the savior of Huntsville and an American Cold War hero. In that same time, he went from overseeing a program of forced labor to championing civil rights and racial integration in Alabama." He went to HBCUs throughout the country to recruit promising Black engineers and scientists.

In 1965, Alabama's white supremacist governor, George C. Wallace, decided to appear at the NASA headquarters in Huntsville with reporters. This was part of Wallace's PR blitz to publicize what he called "the real Alabama," an attempt to eclipse the violence inflicted on Black and white civil rights workers by his supporters. Wallace had physically blocked Black students from enrolling at the University of Alabama, knowing that education would do more to undermine white supremacy than nearly anything else. So now he was attempting to take credit for the efforts to get a man on the moon, and a visit to NASA provided the perfect stage. Von Braun wanted nothing to do with it. In fact, he was prepared to move his entire operation—the loss of $589 million in federal subsidies for the space-research industry in the state. But before that extreme measure was taken, von Braun had another option.

After a big ceremony that included the firing of a Saturn V rocket, von Braun and James Webb, who was the NASA administrator at the time, spoke to the assembled group of press from all over the country and Alabama elected officials, including Wallace. They said that Alabama needed to offer its citizens equal opportunities without reference to their race. In a not-so-subtle reference to slavery, von Braun said, "The era belongs to those who can shed the shackles of the past." The headline of the story in the *New York Times* on June 14, 1965, read, "Von Braun Fights Alabama Racism." And below, "Scientist Warns State U.S. Might Close Space Center." George Wallace never visited Huntsville again. Indeed, many years later in 1982, after having survived an assassination attempt that left him paralyzed from the waist down, Wallace met with civil rights leaders and apologized. In 1987, he even reconciled with Rev. Jesse Jackson. They prayed together.

What to make of people like von Braun and George Wallace? They both represent the human potential for transformation. Von Braun never issued a public apology like Wallace, but both men became advocates, albeit flawed ones, for equality. I am writing this during a period of frightening divisiveness in the United States, and there is darkness that seems to be dominating the motivations of many of our leaders and our citizens once more. I look at these two men who were leaders in darkness but somehow found a path of redemption, and I wonder: What did it take for them to get there? These stories are, for me, sources of inspiration and hope.

What von Braun and others began in Huntsville continued long after his death in 1977. When the Marshall Space Flight Center was established in 1960, Huntsville was fifty-one square miles and home to 72,365 people, 14 percent of whom were Black residents. While the populations of Birmingham, Montgomery, and Mobile have all declined every year, Huntsville just keeps growing. By 2023, Huntsville was the largest city in Alabama, with 235,204 residents—30 percent of whom are Black—but if you include the entire metropolitan area, now a sprawling 1,300 square miles, that population soars to 500,000.

Americans don't fully appreciate my state's contradictions—the odd combination of the reddest Republican stronghold and pockets of remarkable progressivism. Even though I have spent most of my life in Alabama, Huntsville was an outlier even to me. Our politics can be surprising—even baffling. In March 2024, our district elected a Democrat to the Alabama House of Representatives. Marilyn Lands won 62.31 percent of the vote to replace a Republican who had to resign after pleading guilty to voter fraud. It's hard to imagine so decisive a victory happening in another part of the state.

I moved to Huntsville in 2021, during the pandemic. One day, a package for my neighbor was mistakenly delivered to me, and, as it happens, my package was delivered to her. We connected on our neighborhood Facebook page. She told me she'd seen a *60 Minutes* story about me and my environmental justice work and shared that she had grown up in rural Mississippi and was familiar with the problem. She worked at NASA headquarters in Washington,

DC, and her husband worked at the Marshall Space Flight Center in town. From this chance encounter, avenues opened up for our organization to collaborate with NASA.

NASA has become the incubator for innovative uses of technology that made possible not only a moon landing but also many other advancements that have become so woven into our lives we don't even question where they came from. Scratchproof lenses on eyeglasses, for example, or ear thermometers, baby formula, the computer mouse, headphones, smoke detectors, insulation, dust busters, memory foam mattresses, shoe insoles, camera phones, tap water filters, GPS systems, and MRIs—all were initially designed for space travel and then mass-produced.

The catastrophic effects of climate change have also engaged the agency. Since 1979, NASA has charted the rise in carbon dioxide and methane and the concomitant rise in global temperature and the precipitous decline of Arctic Sea ice. In a state filled with climate change deniers, NASA has been an outpost of pure science and troubling data that it is able to harvest from satellites deep in space, chronicling the problems on Earth.

It is also studying ways to mitigate the effects of climate change. One intriguing effort was its use of bacteria—called "biologically assisted electrolysis"—as a source of green power. Once more, there is an overlap with our work. That technology is used to clean up wastewater and to power operations for food and beverage companies.

The efficient disposal of waste is a problem for communities rich and poor, urban and rural the world over. The storied British boarding school Eton, a place that has educated kings and other British elites for centuries, had to close down in January 2024 because flooding in the river Thames so stressed the sewage system that the toilets couldn't function. No one would have ever dreamed that Eton and Jackson, Mississippi, would have something this fundamental in common—nor that astronauts orbiting Earth would be privy, so to speak, to the solution.

When NASA tests rockets for space exploration, I can feel my house shake. I think about these missions that aim to place people in lunar habitats, and I recognize that these places too will need sanitation. With NASA, my organization is working to develop sanitation systems that can work not only on a climate-challenged Earth but also on the dusty landscape of the moon.

What will this look like in the year 2050? I will be old, and my grandchildren will be all grown up. My daughter may be a grandmother herself. I can imagine us sitting on my back deck in the evening, after the sun has set and the dishes from our family dinner are washed. There is my family, looking at the enormous harvest moon lingering over our community, as it does a few times every year.

But this time, we may have the uncanny sense that from the moon, people in their 3D-printed homes are looking at our fragile blue planet. And in those homes, there will be ways of dealing with waste that we helped make possible and that, in turn, helped to make life on that previously inhospitable landscape possible. What will they see when they look at us? Will we have managed to reverse the dire effects of climate change? If we continue on this destructive path, without technological breakthroughs and seismic changes to our fossil fuel economy, the climate crisis will lead to an additional 14.5 million deaths, rising seas, disappearing communities, and climate migration heretofore unseen in history.

Perhaps the people living on the moon will feel grateful to have escaped that fate.

What Reverend Abernathy had hoped for more than fifty years ago feels even more urgent today. And today, it seems that the answer to his question—Would NASA "support the movement to combat the nation's poverty, hunger, and other social problems"?—turned out to be yes.

SEVEN

Holy Ground

ON APRIL 29, 2018, I WENT TO MONTGOMERY, ALABAMA, for the dedication of the National Memorial for Peace and Justice. This was the culmination of an extraordinary project spearheaded by Bryan Stevenson, the founder and executive director of the Equal Justice Initiative, an organization committed to ending mass incarceration, racial inequality, and the draconian punishments that are inherent in our criminal justice system. Bryan understands that changing our carceral system today should not be done in a historical vacuum, ignorant of the racism and the racial violence that inform our country's history. That's why he wanted to bring into existence a project much like the great memorials to those who were murdered in the Holocaust, that would pay tribute to the thousands of Black people who were, in his words, "drowned, burned, shot, and hanged" in the Jim Crow South.

At one point in my career, when I returned to Alabama, I worked for EJI. Bryan first became a mentor and then a close friend, so naturally I joined him and hundreds of others that day in Montgomery for the opening ceremony for the National Memorial. It was the centerpiece of a yearslong, ambitious effort that engaged and educated communities all over the country about the sites of these hideous crimes of racial violence. To start, he and his researchers combed through archives to try to document lynchings that took place between the end of Reconstruction in 1877 and the 1950s. They were able to document 4,400 individuals who lost their lives to racial violence. They located where these unprosecuted crimes took place. They learned as much as they possibly could about the victims. They contacted descendants of the murdered and community leaders where these lynchings took place to arrange memorials at the sites.

On six acres overlooking Montgomery stands an overwhelming structure: eight hundred patinaed columns hang from the roof. They're made from Corten steel, which turns a rusty red when exposed to the elements. On each column is the name of a county, followed by the names of people who were lynched there. In some cases, only "Unknown" marks the loss. Most victims never had a proper burial, and many might have been lost to history—had Bryan and his researchers not discovered them.

In another part of the memorial, we learn stories about the victims. One, Mary Turner, was pregnant when she spoke out against the white mob who had lynched her husband. In response, the mob hung her by her feet, burned her, and then sliced her belly open. The unborn child slipped out, yet another victim with no name and no chance at a peaceful life. Mary was just one of thousands of innocents who'd been slaughtered, with each story more harrowing than the next. In Lowndes County, those older than us remembered a time when relatives, friends, and neighbors were lynched for standing up to white supremacy or demanding fair wages for their labor. At the memorial we could read the details we'd been spared as children.

On that April day, I attended the faith dedication of the soaring memorial. Hundreds of us gathered as ministers, priests, and a rabbi spoke about this national trauma and about healing. There are duplicate steel markers laid out in an adjacent field, where communities may claim the marker for their county to create their own monument back home.

Also on exhibit is a collection of hundreds of glass jars that contain soil from the sites where the violence took place—some of it rich and dark, others various shades of brown, even red. "In the soil is the blood of those who were lynched," Bryan told those in attendance. "In the soil are the tears of those who were humiliated during segregation. But in the soil we have collected, we can plant something. And it can grow. And it can be beautiful, and it can nurture us, and it can feed us and lead us into a new era."

Three years earlier, before the memorial opened, the Equal Justice Initiative had gathered a number of volunteers to launch the project of collecting soil from the lynching sites. Hundreds of us were deployed with glass jars inscribed with the location and the names of victims to gather the soil and return it to Montgomery for inclusion in the exhibit. My friend Lynda, her husband, her son, and I were tasked with collecting dirt from the site where the Powell brothers had been lynched. We were given a glass jar, a small trowel, and the biographical information about the people whose lives had been so brutally cut short. The two young men were murdered for having been "insolent" to a white farmer "after brushing up against his horse on the road." The ensuing argument led to a mob of one hundred white men attacking the brothers and hanging them from a tree.

We returned to Lowndes County and went to the site—an isolated field. We bowed our heads in tribute to these men and started digging. I was acutely aware of the significance of this humble task, of how many backbreaking hours my enslaved ancestors spent digging in Alabama soil, and how their remains may also have been laid to rest there. And of course, I could not help but think of the anguish and terror those two young men must have felt until the moment their souls left their bodies. I glanced at Lynda's son, who was about the same age as the Powell brothers. We carefully filled our jars and screwed on the lids. The only witness was a cow standing in a nearby pasture.

I had heard about instances where the lynchings had taken place on private property, so those who were sent to dig up the soil could be accused of trespassing. In this part of the world, that is nothing to take lightly, so the folks on the soil-collection mission would knock on doors and inform the property owners of the task they wished to complete. In some cases, when the owners learned about the project, they too got on their knees and helped dig up this blood-soaked dirt. A different kind of communion and reconciliation took place. Most of the property owners had no idea what had transpired on the land they called home. When people learn about our country's violent history, they often become more connected, more empathic. Suppressing historic truth seems to me an effort to keep us divided.

A few months after we collected the soil, I was asked to find the Powell family church. EJI wanted to erect a historic marker about the young men, as they did in communities all over the country. I found some Powell family members in Lowndes County and their church in Sandy Springs. One day in July 2016, a small crowd of people stood in the warm rain outside the Rehobeth Missionary Baptist Church, praying. A large blue plaque emblazoned with gold letters states, LYNCHING IN LETOHATCHEE. Then the stories of the seven victims in Letohatchee, Alabama, are laid out. In 1900, Jim Cross, his wife, and their two children were lynched after speaking out against the lynching of another Black man in their community. Two decades later, the marker reads, William Powell and his brother, "whose name was reported as Samuel or Jesse, were also lynched in Letohatchee."

As I stood there, reflecting on these lives that had been so senselessly and brutally lost, I felt grateful to be alive at a time when we could at last recognize what had transpired. I recalled what Bryan had said about the impetus for the project: "We have been silent about lynching for too long. It's time to end the silence, to memorialize those who died, who fled, who feared the terror our nation tolerated."

But there were so many others, not only Black people, who shared a similarly violent history in our country, in Alabama, and in Lowndes County. We are called "Bloody Lowndes" for so many reasons, and the soil that we dug up that day may have contained traces of the blood, the tears, the suffering, not only of

Black people but of our Indigenous sisters and brothers. The soil that had been in my hands held so much of the history of myself and so many others—histories that had been suppressed, histories I wanted to learn and hold too.

WHEN YOU ARE TRAVELING NORTH on Freedom Road and reach the town of White Hall at the intersection with US 80, there is a historic marker on the right, this one with white letters against a black background. "Holy Ground Battlefield," it says. "Six miles North, on December 23, 1813, General F. L. Claiborne's army defeated the Creeks and destroyed the Holy Ground Indian Village. One American was killed and 33 Creeks. William 'Red Eagle' Weatherford escaped by leaping on horseback into the river and swimming across. This defeat closed Creek military operations in South Alabama and facilitated General Jackson's victory at Horseshoe Bend." Like so many instances of recorded history in the South, this is not entirely accurate. Lowndes County is in central—not southern—Alabama. And yet contained in those sixty-four words is a world of tragedy, of myth, of yet another fragment in the intricate and complicated mosaic that makes America, in which the fates of Black, white, and Indigenous peoples are knitted together. Indeed, many people from Lowndes County who grew up with me had some sense that the history of Indigenous people was intertwined with our own. And yet, these frames of reference, these histories, weren't easily accessible to us.

When I was in the tenth grade, my class went on a field trip to Holy Ground Battlefield. As we all climbed on the bus, we had assumed we were going to the recreational area we all knew. For us, what once was a battlefield was now a park right on the Alabama River constructed by the Army Corps of Engineers. It had a kiosk about birding, a swimming area, secluded spaces with grills where people could barbeque and picnic, and lots of trails. As the name reveals, and we later learned, it was once holy ground for the Red Stick Creeks, though my classmates and I saw little visible evidence of its spiritual importance. As we wandered around the site, though, our teacher told us the story of the battle and what had happened to the Creeks. When we got to the overlook at the Alabama River, we marveled at the leap William "Red Eagle" Weatherford had taken on his horse to escape.

I can't recall if I felt it then, but over the years, the spiritual importance of that area became ever more profound to me. It was originally a hallowed place for the Creeks, a center for their community, and then was overwritten as a site of combat and annihilation. Finally, it became a spot for elementary and high school expeditions, Alabama tourists, and family excursions—a stark contrast with the grim realities of the area's glorious and tragic past. Even before I fully learned its history, I had the sense that the roots of the African American population ran deep within the blood-drenched soil of Lowndes County, but the roots of the Indigenous tribes that lived there ran deeper still—before they were violently severed.

What I couldn't anticipate, as a teenager, was how Holy Ground would become consequential in my own life—even as only a few members of the Creek Nation remained in my community. I kept returning to Holy Ground; something kept pulling me back there. I did not know anything about my history, which I would only learn decades later. I didn't know about my own entangled connections to the Indigenous people, the enslaved Africans, and even the enslavers who fought the battle. Still, Holy Ground drew me like an undertow I couldn't explain.

Twelve years after that school field trip, in 1985, when it was time for me to marry, we held the ceremony at Holy Ground. Whenever I needed a moment to pause and reflect after my return to Lowndes County, I would drive there and walk to the river or sit silently on one of the benches. In 2015, when my life as an environmental activist had fully taken shape, I worked with the Center for Earth Ethics, an organization founded by former vice president Al Gore's daughter Karenna and based out of Union Theological Seminary. It links faith, ethics, and the environment. We decided to organize what has become known as a "climate training" in Lowndes County, an opportunity for local people to recognize the impact of climate change in their community and then figure out practical strategies to address it locally. At the beginning of the training, we sought a shared experience that would bring our group together, and I knew instantly that it would have to take place at Holy Ground. What I hadn't expected was that it would change my life.

I HAD BEEN CURIOUS about Indigenous people since I was a child. My mother referred to her grandmother as having been an Indigenous woman. My gym teacher in high school insisted that I must have had "Indian blood." I had long wanted to learn more about the Indigenous history of Lowndes County, and gradually I did. Fierce battles had taken place between the white European colonizers and the Indigenous people who had lived there for centuries. The Cherokee, Choctaw, Chickasaw, Creek, and Seminole Nations were known as the Five Civilized Tribes, as they all had, to a certain extent, assimilated to the culture of the white settlers. They became Christian and spoke English, and some of them participated in the slave trade and enslaved Black people. In the early part of the nineteenth century, the land that would eventually become Lowndes County was governed by the Muscogee (Creek) Nation, whose citizens lived throughout the Southwest.

In *A Conquering Spirit: Fort Mims and the Redstick War of 1813–1814*, the anthropologist Gregory A. Waselkov recounts the long history of Creeks interacting with Europeans, which preceded even the Revolutionary War. In what he described as the "demographic chaos of the seventeenth century," which included the Dutch, Spaniards, other Europeans, and a variety of other native tribes, there emerged "colliding interests of four peoples: settlers of European descent, the Native American Creeks, African Americans (held in slavery by both whites and Indians), and the mixed-race offspring of the other three."

Colliding interests also took place within the Creek Nation. During the War of 1812, two conflicting internal factions emerged: one, known as the Red Sticks, were in favor of securing dominance of the region by overpowering the colonists in physical warfare. Their name came from their use of red sticks as weapons. The other group of Creeks were more inclined to assimilate with European culture—they engaged in commerce and cooperation with the settlers, and there was some intermarriage. It didn't take long for these two opposing visions of their identity to clash, and in 1813, a civil war within the Creek Nation began.

The white colonists observing this conflict panicked and moved into a fort that was on the property owned by the colonist Samuel Mims. Emboldened by their successes in combat, the Red Sticks—led by two chiefs with the unusually British names of Peter McQueen and William "Red Eagle" Weatherford—attacked the fort. Settlers, some enslaved people, mixed-blood Creeks, and others who had sought refuge in Fort Mims were massacred. In the complicated stew of the status of enslaved people at the time, some of the Black people who were involved were freed, others remained enslaved, and many were taken captive. Hundreds of people were killed and the property was burned. The massacre eroded any promise of peaceful coexistence between settlers and Indigenous people, creating a contagion of fear that spread throughout the region.

Over the summer and into the fall following the Battle of Fort Mims, the Red Stick Creeks created three different encampments, secured in ways that were comparable to military forts—but with one big distinction: a spiritual component. One of the encampments, a village, was located in Lowndes County, right on the bluffs of the Alabama River. The area was called Econochaca, a Creek word that means "holy ground." It had been sanctified by Josiah Francis, a special leader who was known as a Creek prophet. Among the ceremonies he performed was one believed to create a protective spiritual perimeter around the area—in this case specifically against white men. Those who attempted to trespass would be killed. Prophet Francis had spearheaded a radical movement among many Creeks to reject the association with white culture and embrace their former traditional customs and identities. Their community included some Black men and women who had been enslaved at Fort Mims and freed after the attack.

Meanwhile, having suffered such a catastrophic defeat at the hands of the Creeks, the local military bolstered their reserves of fighters, including members of other tribes like the Choctaws, for decisive retaliation. General Ferdinand Claiborne, who commanded the Mississippi Territory militia during the War of 1812, systematically expanded his forces over the autumn months following the attack on Fort Mims. By November, he had mobilized about 1,200 soldiers to attack the Creeks at Holy Ground. The Creeks got wind of this planned offense, and William "Red Eagle" Weatherford mobilized his 350 warriors and evacuated the women and children from the settlement. In December of 1813, mere months after the Creeks' great victory, Claiborne's soldiers took Holy Ground. Around thirty of the Indigenous warriors and African American men were killed, while the others escaped. Weatherford, astride his horse while surrounded by hostile gunfire, famously leapt off a fifteen-foot-high bluff into the Alabama River, enshrining a legend of fearlessness that is forever connected to his name. Following their victory, Claiborne's men ransacked the camp, and their Choctaw allies burned the village to the ground.

This was the beginning of the end of the Creek people in Lowndes County. The Battle of Holy Ground became a catalyst for subsequent forced removals that marked the commencement of the government's inhumane Indian Removal Policy, culminating in the tragedy of the Trail of Tears. Eventually, twenty-three million acres of land that the Creek people once claimed as their own, consisting of around half of Alabama and parts of southern

Georgia—was surrendered to the white settlers. With the signing of the Indian Removal Act in 1830—considered today as a government-sanctioned act of genocide, forcible property removal, and ethnic cleansing—President Andrew Jackson forced as many as a hundred thousand Native Americans to give up their homes, their tribal lands, and a culture that had been theirs long before the arrival of white settlers. Federal troops were summoned to violently enforce their relocation to a region called Indian Country, located west of the Mississippi River. In 1834, about fifty Creek towns in the area were dissolved and over a ten- to twelve-year period 23,000 Creeks were forced to march over unforgiving land, a trek that was marked by epic levels of starvation, disease, and death. The paths they walked became testimony to the cruelty of displacement, another tragic chapter in the history of this country.

IN MY EARLY ENCOUNTERS with Holy Ground, I felt an inexplicable pull, a connection that transcended time. Holy Ground spoke to me, not just for its historic significance but as a place steeped in the struggles, resilience, and spirituality of Indigenous peoples. It also spoke to me because these were the lands of my parents' ancestors. My Coleman ancestors, my father's people, had lived not far from where the Creek Wars took place. And my mother's people, the Debardelabens, came from right across the Alabama River. When William "Red Eagle" Weatherford and his horse leapt into the river, they literally crossed from my father's lands to my mother's.

When I first got married, in July 1985, I insisted that we have the ceremony on the Holy Ground lands. It was such a beautiful corner of the world that it needed no decoration. Moss hung like gauze curtains from the trees, butterflies seemed to be everywhere, and at the overhang you could look out on the Alabama River. It had the quality of a secret, enchanted, sacred space. My fiancé didn't care where we got married, but I was drawn to the place for the great sense of peace that I felt when I was there. If I could have been baptized in a river, this is the site I would have chosen.

We made our vows in a gazebo overlooking the river. There was a wooden walkway that led from the street, bordered by trees draped with moss, and my brother, who later became a minister, walked me down the aisle. My father had given us his blessing. It was not a big wedding. Indeed, it was pretty much improvised. My fiancé was in the military, stationed in Oklahoma, so we had to head out there shortly after the ceremony, no time for a honeymoon. In retrospect, there is some painful irony in our journey: we went from the Creeks' holy ground to the place where they were exiled after they'd been forced to walk the Trail of Tears.

In what felt like several lifetimes later, in 2015, I attended a ceremony at the Edmund Pettus Bridge commemorating the fiftieth anniversary of the historic march from Selma to Montgomery. It was a thrill to be in the crowd when President Barack Obama and First Lady Michelle Obama arrived in their presidential limousine. I felt especially honored to see President Obama push the wheelchair of Amelia Boynton Robinson, at 103 years old, across the bridge. She and Representative John R. Lewis—who was also there—were beaten and tear-gassed by law enforcement as they and hundreds of others tried to cross the bridge on March 7, 1965. The black-and-white photograph of Amelia Boynton Robinson, who had been an organizer of the march, was seared in my memory. Not only mine—when it was published, this iconic image of a well-dressed, dignified Black woman, battered and bruised, so weakened by the assault that she needed to be held up by two other well-dressed Black people, came to embody the violent injustices in the South.

I remember watching the events commemorating the anniversary of the march while sharing a blanket on the grass with Karenna Gore. Like her father, Karenna is an impassioned advocate for the environment, and as someone with both a law degree and a divinity degree from Union Theological Seminary, she brings a spiritual dimension to her work. During Climate Week in 2014, she had organized a conference in New York City called "Religions for the Earth," which gathered over two hundred global religious and spiritual leaders to, in her words, "reframe climate change as a moral issue and galvanize faith-based action to address it." The success of this led her to start the Center for Earth Ethics at Union Theological Seminary. Our time together at Edmund Pettus Bridge marked the beginning of one of my most significant friendships and professional relationships.

Later, when I visited her in New York, we immediately fell into a conversation about Indigenous history, connecting deeply around Indigenous wisdom and climate change. I told her that among the areas I'd studied for my master's degree in history—including European history and the history of the Holocaust—was American civil rights history and the history of Indigenous people. My work in Lowndes County was gaining some greater attention, and I felt it was important to help our residents understand their own ability to help make a difference in their immediate environment, even if they could not install sophisticated septic systems to cope with the waste. So together we organized what is known as a climate training in White Hall, a town in Lowndes County that is adjacent to Holy Ground, to figure out ways to get ordinary people to work on local solutions to the climate crisis.

When we organized the training, I insisted that we include an Indigenous earth-honoring ceremony, led by an Indigenous leader. I wanted to bring people to the sacred space I knew so well. We were so fortunate to engage Lyla June Johnston, a poet affiliated with the Center for Humans and Nature, whose lineages are Navajo and Cheyenne. Steeped in academic knowledge—she graduated with honors from Stanford University with a degree in environmental anthropology—she brings an intellectual heft to her commitment to revitalizing our spiritual relationship with Mother Earth.

She was joined by Mindahi Bastida, a member of the Otomi-Toltec peoples who live mostly in the Mexican state of Hidalgo. Mindahi worked closely with Karenna and was the director of the Original Caretakers program at the Center for Earth Ethics. He had a long career with UNESCO and other UN programs, focusing on sacred sites and environmental justice. His wife, Geraldine Patrick Encina, who has Mapuche and Celtic ancestry, specializes in ethnoecology, in which she immerses in fascinating studies of the astronomical and ecological foundations of how people in Mesoamerica charted time. (Their daughter, Xiye, has become a globally recognized climate activist.) There could not have been better people to lead us in this ritual. I had gotten to know them before this meeting, and they were instrumental in helping me understand my own Indigenous background.

About fifty of us gathered very early in the morning on Holy Ground, very near to the spot where I had been married decades before. So much had changed in my life since then. In a winding path, filled with generous guides and remarkable interventions, I had found my passion and my mission on this planet. I looked around at the people who had joined us. They were from all over the state. Even a caretaker who worked in the park was with us. Standing near the edge of the Alabama River, Lyla June asked that we pick up some of the earth, which we cradled in our hands. Then she told us to form a circle, with our eyes closed, while Mindahi, Geraldine, and Lyla June stood in the middle. We then turned and acknowledged the four directions, north, south, east, and west, before we settled into a vast silence. The peace felt as if it inhabited my entire body.

Then the earth in my hands felt as if it had sprung to life, moving as if it were filled with energy. I thought that I had picked up soil that was crawling with worms, the activity was so intense. I stayed true to the ceremony and kept my eyes closed. If there were worms in my hands, so be it. I would find out later. At the same moment, the air was filled with the sound of fish jumping in the water. A flock of birds flew overhead, and we could hear them singing. All of this occurred simultaneously as I held this vibrant bit of earth in my hands, so alive and active. Like the soil collections we did for EJI that held the blood of martyred Black men, women, and children, so too was the soil at Holy Ground filled with blood, with tears, with the sweat of our forebears. In church we talk about the power of the blood, meaning the blood of Christ. Here, I discovered the power of the soil.

As we opened our eyes, we were asked to identify who we were. And as we went around the circle, it turned out that everyone had some Indigenous heritage, including the caretaker—who I had assumed was white. When it was my turn, I said, "Muscogee." The Creeks are part of the Muscogee Nation. At that point I had done my DNA test and had engaged in probing conversations with Lyla June, Mindahi, and Geraldine. We had spoken in New York and in some private moments after they arrived; they helped educate me about my connections with my Indigenous history, so I felt confident in my declaration.

The stories unfolded before us and only further connected us to one another, to the experience, and to the world around us. The final act was sharing the peace pipe (this was just before COVID). Tobacco is very much a part of these ceremonies, so we inhaled and passed the pipe around. Many people believe that if you weren't born and raised and socialized within a tribe, it is presumptuous, a kind of cultural appropriation, to connect with our Indigenous ancestors. But there are connections that are ineffable, ones I can't explain. In every sense of the word, mystical as it may sound, these ties are spiritual.

I AM A CHRISTIAN and have spent quite a lot of time in churches. I've often experienced the movement of the Spirit passing through me. There have been times when I felt, in a very personal way, the presence of Jesus providing comfort. But even with my foundational knowledge and encounters with the important traditions and spirituality of my Christian faith, the only times I have ever felt a similar power have been during Indigenous ceremonies. I felt that power on the banks of the Alabama River. I felt it too in 2016, at the Cannonball River with the Standing Rock Sioux Tribe, where I protested the violation of their sacred lands and the contamination of their water by the fossil fuel industry.

Holding the grainy earth, from the holy ground of the Red Stick Creeks, I felt a power beyond my understanding raining down on us, embracing us, making us one with the earth. So much of my work as a climate activist focuses on the devastation and the danger we've inflicted on this planet. But that moment reminded me in important ways of the vast and mysterious beauties of what we are fighting for and our interconnectedness. I felt it when I dug the earth around the site where the Powell brothers had been lynched, and also that day with my fellow activists in that circle, and also with the birds and the trees and the living, miraculous soil vibrating in my hands. Ashes to ashes, dust to dust, the Bible tells us, and I wondered if this earth might have contained the remains of Indigenous peoples who had been buried in that sacred ground. Perhaps my own Indigenous and Black ancestors. Is this what it all comes to? If so, then we are blessed and eternal in ways that I had never imagined.

EIGHT

This Is What
Disinvestment Looks Like

OVER THE YEARS, I'VE BEEN TO JACKSON, MISSISSIPPI, THE state's capital, many times, in my many lives as a teacher, an advocate for civil rights, a speaker, and an environmental and climate justice activist. In my family, Mississippi loomed large as a place of special menace, even in the Jim Crow South. For as long as I can remember, my father would refer to the 1955 murder of Emmett Till, the fourteen-year-old boy from Chicago whose visit to his grandparents in the Mississippi Delta resulted in a historic tragedy. For the alleged "crime" of talking to a white woman, Emmett was mutilated, beaten, tortured, and shot, and his broken, dead body was dumped into the Tallahatchie River. His mother made sure the world saw what these racists had wrought by demanding her son's broken body be seen, sharing the image with *Life* magazine. What happened to Emmett Till gained the power of a terrifying myth, or a cautionary tale: Don't dare transgress even in the slightest, because this is what could happen to you.

But for my father and civil rights activists like him, the martyrdom of Emmett Till encapsulated the racial violence and injustice they devoted their lives to defeating. Mississippi became a place of immense historic significance, and over the years, it produced more than its share of notable individuals, among them Medgar and Myrlie Evers; Ross Barnett; James Meredith, who integrated Ole Miss in 1962; Fannie Lou Hamer; and, much later, Oprah Winfrey.

In 1988 I accepted an invitation to visit Jackson from an important Mississippi civil rights icon, Lawrence Guyot. Guyot had been a member of the Student Nonviolent Coordinating Committee (SNCC) and president of the Mississippi Freedom Democratic Party. His memories ran deep. We met at a discussion of the film *Mississippi Burning* in Washington, DC, where I was working as a teacher. The film recounted another chapter in the Civil Rights Movement, a terrifying period during which he had played a significant role.

The film tells the story of the 1964 murder of three civil rights workers—James Chaney, who was African American, and Andrew Goodman and Michael Schwerner, who were white and Jewish, as they were working to register voters throughout the South as a part of the Freedom Summer campaign. At the time, Lawrence Guyot was a twenty-five-year-old organizer with Mississippi's Freedom Movement. Guyot joined the organization in 1961—only six years after Till's murder, when life in the state was filled with menace for Black people—while he was a student at Tougaloo College, an HBCU located in Jackson. He became the director of the Congress of Racial Equality (CORE) project in Hattiesburg, a community in the southern part of the state, about two hours south of where Chaney, Schwerner, and Goodman were working.

Chaney, Goodman, and Schwerner were arrested over a bogus traffic violation. After being detained for several hours, they were released, and they started driving away. In their rearview mirror, they could see they were being tailed by the police. This time the danger was profound. I know those often-desolate Mississippi country roads, and I certainly know the overwhelming power white police officers once held—indeed still do.

The cars arrived in Neshoba County, a place where the earth was drenched with the blood of enslaved and Indigenous people. This area was once the ancestral home of the Choctaw, who in the 1830s were among the first native people forcibly relocated by President Andrew Jackson's Indian Removal program. The three young men were apprehended, driven to another location, and shot at close range. But who pulled the trigger? Who else was involved?

Once the burned-out car the men had driven was discovered, FBI agents were sent into the area to investigate. The timing was propitious: violence was tearing through the South, racial justice activists had become more prominent, and there was a sympathetic president, Lyndon Johnson, in the White House. The investigation expanded to include local and state authorities and even four hundred US sailors. It was a huge operation, given more propulsion, perhaps, by the fact that two of the men who died were white northerners. Seven weeks later, the men's bodies were discovered in an earthen dam—a levee built along the edges of a stream to prevent flooding of land. With evidence of a close-range murder, the investigation intensified, and soon members of the KKK, the local sheriff's office, and the Philadelphia, Mississippi, police department were implicated.

But this was Mississippi in 1964, after all, and the state still had enormous discretion in how to proceed. It refused to prosecute the alleged perpetrators of this ghastly crime. I can only imagine how all those white men had friends and family members and business connections that shot straight through the state legislature and into the offices first of Governor Ross Robert Barnett and then later Governor Paul B. Johnson Jr.—both segregationist Democrats, by the way, as was the state legislature at the time.

Only in 1967, after the Department of Justice leveled federal charges, were eighteen people held accountable of civil rights violations. A jury of their peers, however, was lenient: only seven men were convicted. All were given minor sentences by a benevolent judge. But history rhymes, as they say, and in 2005, one of the men, Edgar Ray Killen, was charged by the state of Mississippi, convicted of three counts of manslaughter, and sentenced to sixty years in prison—his time served was abbreviated by his death in 2018.

The film was named after the case file, "Mississippi Burning." My students were riveted by the true crime aspects and the powerful historic resonance. I had educated these young people, who came of age during the Reagan administration, about the enormity of what was at stake during the Civil Rights Movement. Several weeks earlier, we'd traveled to Alabama and marched from Selma to Montgomery to commemorate the twenty-fifth anniversary of that historic event. After the screening, they had the privilege of asking Lawrence Guyot, who'd lived this history, what it all meant. Guyot patiently answered their questions: Were you afraid? Did you ever see a Klansman? Was the movie accurate? Yes, yes, and yes.

Afterward, Guyot invited me and my students to come to Jackson to commemorate the anniversary of the Mississippi Congressional Challenge, where they would meet people who'd participated in the event in 1965. Naturally, I accepted. The greatest gift that I could give my students was the power of historical knowledge, and whenever there was a chance for them to experience it firsthand, I seized the opportunity.

We held fundraisers and bake sales and persuaded the school to part with some funds, and then we boarded the bus for the fifteen-hour drive. Once we arrived, we attended events at numerous locations, including the campus of the storied HBCU Jackson State University, founded in 1877.

The culmination of the visit took place at the governor's mansion, where Governor William A. Allain had invited those who had served in the Student Nonviolent Coordinating Committee and members of the Mississippi Freedom Democratic Party to attend. On January 4, 1965, when the Eighty-Ninth US Congress was called into session, these brave men and women traveled to Washington to object to the swearing in of the delegation from Mississippi. They had attempted to get Fannie Lou Hamer, Annie Devine, and Victoria Gray on the November ballot as Independents, but their effort was blocked by the Mississippi State Board of Elections. The MFDP filed a formal challenge to the election with the House of Representatives.

When they received no response within the thirty-day period, they traveled to Washington, DC, to confront members of

Congress. Since all demonstrations inside the Capitol buildings are forbidden, the demonstrators gathered in the underground tunnels. They were impossible to ignore. Stokely Carmichael, by then a leading figure in the movement, described that day:

> On opening day, as congressmen and their aides made their way through these tunnels, they turned a corner and found themselves passing between two lines of silent, working [B]lack men and women from Mississippi. The people, spaced about ten feet apart, stood still as statues, dignified, erect, utterly silent. . . . The congressmen had come by in little groups, each group, a congressman and one or two aides, deep in conversation. They'd turn the corner, and for a moment the sight of our people would stop them dead in their tracks. We didn't move or say a mumbling word. Then the group would walk between the two rows, but now suddenly very silent. It's hard to describe the power of that moment.

This was before the passage of the Voting Rights Act of 1965, but clearly this demonstration was one more step in bringing the deprivation of these rights to the public's attention.

At the governor's mansion, more than twenty years later, many of those who had lined the underground tunnels of Congress stood around a large table and sang "Oh Freedom!"

> Oh freedom, oh freedom
> Oh freedom all over me

And before I be a slave
I'll be buried in my grave
And go on to my Lord and be free

Everyone was moved to tears—but the men and women who'd fought the fight were quite overwhelmed by this invitation from the governor and what it represented.

Many of these heroes of the movement have since passed away, including Lawrence Guyot, who died only two weeks after President Barack Obama was reelected in 2012. It is almost a blessing that they aren't here to witness what has happened to our country since that special day in 1988. I can imagine them crying today for different reasons. What would they make of Jackson, Mississippi, today?

Today, Jackson is the embodiment of neglect, of a collapsing infrastructure, of environmental injustice at its most extreme. Families have been left without sufficient water pressure to flush toilets. Students must attend school virtually because of the failing and inadequate water and sanitation infrastructure. Cancer patients have been asked to leave hospitals because the water conditions are unsafe. These are the circumstances in a capital city— unheard of in the rest of America. And it is preposterous that when the water crisis in Jackson reached extreme levels, the current occupant of the governor's mansion and the state legislature flat out refused to intervene.

This capital city is an urban version of the rural divide I have observed throughout my life. Just as residents of rural communities contend with little to no infrastructure, so too do the mostly African American residents of Jackson. Just as rural communities must cope with contaminated water and substandard sewage systems, so too do residents of Jackson. In these communities, such urgent needs become easy to ignore by those in power. And the residents too often must accept these monumental wrongs as grim facts of life. Until, that is, they say, "Enough."

AT THE END OF NOVEMBER 2023, I was invited to attend a conference in Jackson sponsored by *The Atlantic* magazine. In partnership with *Mississippi Today*, a local nonprofit news organization, *The Atlantic* had chosen Jackson as the site of "State of Our Union: Mississippi." Its intent, a year before the 2024 presidential election, was to bring together people from the Deep South to explore the transformation and the complex challenges of the region.

Jackson is often referred to as the "Blackest City in America," because African Americans comprise more than 80 percent of its population. Overall, however, its population has been declining. From 2000 to 2010, 19,485 white residents left the city, while 7,976 Black residents settled there—and the population dropped 5.8 percent in that period, from 184,256 in 2000 to 173,514 in 2010. By 2023 there were fewer than 150,000 residents. Once, white people made up half the city's population; now they make up around 15 percent. It hardly seems like a coincidence that this city's infrastructure is on the verge of collapse. How can you build a capital city without resilient infrastructure?

One person tasked with reversing that decline is Chokwe Antar Lumumba, who was sworn in as mayor of Jackson in 2017 when he was just thirty-four years old. Lumumba was born and raised in Jackson, and both of his parents were local activists. Indeed, his

father, who changed his name to Chokwe Lumumba after join-
ing the Black nationalist organization Republic of New Afrika
in 1969, also served as mayor of the city, from July 2013 until he
passed away from a heart ailment less than seven months later.

After Lumumba Sr.'s death, his son and namesake tried to succeed him. He lost that first election, only to score a decisive victory
three years later. He vowed that Mississippi's capital, in the midst
of one of the reddest states in the country, with the Trump administration in the White House, would become "the most radical city
on the planet." As the *Clarion-Ledger*, the local paper of record,
wrote, "To some, Lumumba isn't expected to merely disrupt the
status quo. He's expected to shatter it."

He had such soaring ambitions for this city. Of course, fix-
ing potholes and making city hall responsive to the community
are time-honored parts of good government. But Lumumba also
wanted to implement universal basic income, an urban gardening
project, and alternatives to policing. One recurring theme in this
Black Democratic stronghold was the state government's efforts
to take over various services—local schools, for example—and
more recently there has been a huge power struggle over the mu-
nicipal water supply and infrastructure.

For Lumumba, these conflicts are representative of the state's
efforts to undermine the will of the voters: "An effort to seize control of a Black city run by Black leadership," he said, to which the
response should be "unequivocal in our rejection of it." The state's
interference is all the more remarkable given that Lumumba
managed to secure a $600 million water-improvement allocation
from the EPA. Throughout his tenure—and he has been deci-
sively reelected—the Republican statehouse and governor have

withheld meaningful assistance in terms of coping with the water crisis, as a way to pressure Jackson to surrender control. The NAACP filed a Title VI civil rights complaint in 2022, accusing the governor and legislature of "systematically depriving Jackson the funds that it needs to operate and maintain its water facilities in a safe and reliable manner." As *Politico* pointed out in a 2021 profile of him as he was preparing for his successful reelection campaign, "He's spent more time bailing the city out of its problems than forging new paths."

On my way to Jackson for the conference, I noticed the mayor boarding the plane. When we were waiting for our luggage, I introduced myself. I told him that while I was in Jackson, I hoped to learn more about the water issues that had plagued the city. What he then said framed the narrative of what I would see during my time there. "What you will see in Jackson is *dis*investment," he explained. "That is what we are dealing with."

The morning of the conference, I had arranged to be taken around Jackson, and as we drove through the city, I saw the mayor's observation in real time. The city is a case study of the many-layered impacts of disinvestment versus investment. This is what happens when infrastructure is built that is neither resilient nor sustainable, and when a state legislature and governor from one party seem determined to punish a community dominated by a different party—not to mention a different race.

JACKSON IS THE EMBODIMENT of how environmental inequity and climate change inevitably occupy the same space, and it's an example of the effects of climate change exacerbating failing infrastructure. Natural disasters force us to think about the diffuse harm and damage caused by systemic neglect and unlivable environments over a period of time. Why don't we see and respond to this long-term deterioration with the same kind of urgency we bring to natural disasters?

The construction of Jackson's largest source of drinking water, the Ross Barnett Reservoir, was completed in 1963—two years before the voting-rights demonstrations and the same year as the death of President John F. Kennedy. If you look at the history of hydroelectric power throughout the South, it is one of the government and industry simply taking people's land in order to build reservoirs. It is common knowledge in the community that if you were on a boat in the reservoir, you could look into the water and see the remains of former residents' homes. Naturally, the owners of the purloined land were overwhelmingly poor and Black and they couldn't afford to fight back.

Even without the dubious acquisition of the land, the Ross Barnett Reservoir was troubled from the beginning. On October 5, 1963, the front page of the *Clarion-Ledger* announced, "Dam Sluice Gates Are Open for Ross Barnett Reservoir," in order "to help clear up sewage pollution in the Pearl River below Jackson." This foreshadowed decades of misery for the communities in the area. When the river flooded, it overflowed the dam and inundated low-lying communities with sewage pollution. Fifty years later, the problems created by the Pearl River flooding remain.

Engineers walked away with a paycheck, and the residents were left holding the bag.

In 1993, the city's primary water plant, the O. B. Curtis Water Treatment Plant, was built near the reservoir, and there it remained without sufficient upgrades for twenty years. The young woman who drove me around on my recent visit described the copper-colored water that poured out of her grandmother's faucet. Her grandmother was so resigned to the fact that her tap water was unsafe that boiling it was simply a fact of life. She was not alone. Residents of Jackson routinely must boil their water to ensure its safety—that is, when the pipes have not collapsed and there is water available to boil.

In 2010, several water mains broke during an intense winter storm and, in what can only be attributed to unabashed racism, state officials blocked efforts—such as new bond issues or local sales taxes—to fix the problems that created the mess in the first place. This has been a recurring dynamic over the years: the water system collapses in some way, residents are left in dire straits, and state officials refuse to intervene, while the city loses its tax base, its appeal to investors, and its capacity to retain a vibrant multi-generational community. You must invest in resilience for cities to be resilient.

Another water main break in 2016 that officials did not, or could not, repair for seven years left a massive ditch filled with water next to a golf course. Every few years, another water catastrophe paralyzed the city. From January until March of 2020, Jackson was inundated with a record amount of rainfall, which the sewage system could not withstand. Nearly a half billion—yes, with a *b*—gallons of raw or barely treated sewage ended up in the

Pearl River. Mayor Lumumba, the city council, and a bipartisan group of state legislators devised a plan for collecting overdue payments without bankrupting residents as a way to provide some funds to address the failing water system. The bill passed the state legislature only to be vetoed by Governor Tate Reeves. "Other cities have issues too, why should only Jackson get a carve-out?" he asked. "There are needy Mississippians who would rather not pay their bills all over."

And here is where the water problem becomes an environmental justice crisis. When we pay for our water, we pay not just for what circulates in our homes but also sewage and stormwater costs. Over the years, only the cost of health care has increased more than the cost of water. In poor cities with degraded water systems, low-income residents are burdened with overwhelmingly expensive water bills.

Consider what happened in Michigan, where since 1980, the average cost of water service increased by 285 percent in Detroit and 320 percent in Flint, the site of another notorious water failure. Back in Detroit in 2014, poor and low-income people were unable to keep up with these rising costs and ended up with their water being shut off if their bills were more than sixty days overdue or if they owed more than $150. As consumers sank into catastrophic debt, there was no plan to help those who could not pay. Utilities often put liens on homes for unpaid water bills, a situation that became known as "water mortgages." I know of people who owed so much money to their water company that they were evicted and the utility claimed ownership. Plus, a home without water service can be condemned by city authorities and demolished. Only after a lawsuit filed by the ACLU and the NAACP in

July 2020 did the city of Detroit address the problem with subsidies and caps on charges. But in the meantime, how many people suffered? One estimate said more than twenty thousand homes had their water cut off.

In Jackson, the decayed infrastructure was further disabled by the extreme weather. Yet another freak winter storm hit in 2021. Pipes burst, water mains were rendered useless, and freezing temperatures left residents without water for over a month. Yet again, efforts to secure funding to address the problem were stonewalled by the governor and state legislature, even though Mayor Lumumba was requesting $47 million to provide only essential repairs and improvements. In August 2022, unusually heavy rainfall caused the Pearl River to flood, and once more the crumbling infrastructure collapsed. Again, parts of the city had no running water, while the rest of the city lived under a boil-water notice. The water pressure was so low that it was impossible to take a shower or flush a toilet.

Football legend Deion Sanders was head coach of the Jackson State University football team at the time. "We don't have water. Water means we don't have air-conditioning. We can't use toilets. We don't have water, therefore we don't have ice, which pretty much places a burden on the program," he said. "So right now, we are operating in a crisis mode." He didn't just move the entire team off campus; he moved them all out of town just so they could have showers, water, and food. According to Governor Reeves, the city didn't have "reliable running water at scale." What that meant, Reeves explained, was "the city cannot produce enough water to fight fires, to reliably flush toilets, and to meet other critical needs." And yet, he and the state legislature—overwhelmingly white and Republican—blocked the essential funds for repairing the system.

Only a few months later, during Jackson State University's homecoming game, a time when thousands of people descend on the city, the water system nearly collapsed under the strain. Mayor Lumumba warned the local community to ration their water consumption the following weekend, when another big game was scheduled. "Don't use more than what you need to use, as increased demand at our water treatment facilities could actually cause challenges with our water pressure," he said. "And if the water pressure drops significantly enough, then we might find ourselves in a citywide boil-water notice again."

That's when the federal government finally intervened. President Joe Biden declared a ninety-day state of emergency and authorized federal funds to cover the costs. Later that year, the Department of Justice alleged that Jackson had failed to comply with the Safe Drinking Water Act, and, in a settlement, a federal court order appointed what was referred to as an "interim third-party manager" of the water system. Jackson should also have received tens of millions of dollars from the American Rescue Plan Act for its water systems; in May 2023, the Southern Poverty Law Center filed a complaint to the US Department of the Treasury, alleging that the state legislature again made it nearly impossible for the city to access the funds they needed.

When I met Mayor Lumumba at the airport in late 2023, a year had passed since the state of emergency. Ted Henifin, an engineer and fellow with the nonprofit US Water Alliance, had been appointed as the interim manager and managed to stabilize the system, finally repairing the network of broken valves and pipes that burst so predictably. To make the water system sustainable, some of the financial burden had to be carried by consumers. But in a low-income community, this placed a great burden on those who could least afford it—problems with the water supply still persisted, and community members were also frustrated with the lack of transparency, information, or input they had in the process of resolving the water crisis.

Why would officials in Mississippi allow their capital city to die? The answer might be the fact that Jackson has long had a large, progressive Black population. What's happening in Jackson is not armed combat; it is a slow-motion assault. How does this serve the state of Mississippi? Starving a capital city suggests that your state is not a good place for investment. It is a billboard for inequality. It is a vivid and terrible illustration of the collision course of climate change, racial and income inequity, and partisan politics.

In my closing remarks at the conference, I said, "I think that we're still fighting the Civil War, and people here in Mississippi understand what I'm talking about." There was a kind of rustle of appreciation in the room. "We've replaced a slave economy with a fossil-fuel-based economy. Both of them were inhumane. And we have to find a way out."

NINE

For the Love of My People

I HAVE ALWAYS FELT A SPECIAL CONNECTION TO THE Lowndes County Interpretive Center, a commemorative site on the Selma to Montgomery National Historic Trail that tells the story of the Civil Rights Movement in my community. For those of us who grew up in Lowndes County, the trail was Highway 80, the dangerous route between Selma and Montgomery where our parents, relatives, friends, and friends of friends marched to secure voting rights after the passage of the historic (and now increasingly gutted) Voting Rights Act. During the voting-rights marches of 1965, white people on the side of the road would yell insults and racist threats. Back then, about 15,400 people lived in Lowndes County, with eighty-six white families owning 90 percent of the land. Naturally, they also controlled every part of the government—from mayor to sheriff to the head of schools. This kind of minority rule was easy to secure and sustain if you used violent voter suppression, which, it being Alabama in the 1960s, they did.

We lived in Montgomery, though my father was a native of Lowndes County and we would eventually return there in 1968. My parents were active during the turbulent years of the Civil Rights Movement. The movement for justice at that time consumed the whole region. My mother's family was from Autauga County, just across the Alabama River, and they too were caught up in peaceful protests that often turned violent and dangerous.

In June 1967, after he had stepped down as the head of the Student Nonviolent Coordinating Committee (SNCC) to focus his efforts on the organizing for Freedom Summer, civil rights activist Stokely Carmichael and nine others were arrested in Prattville, the county seat of Autauga County, and charged with "disorderly conduct" by white officers. He was held "incommunicado," as a local civil rights newsletter put it, in the Prattville jail. Apparently, they overheard him having the audacity to say the words "Black power." One of the other people who had been arrested was a close friend of my parents, John Jackson, who went on to become the mayor for more than three decades of White Hall, a rural Lowndes County town located along the Selma to Montgomery Trail that was a hotbed of activism during the voting-rights movement. It was also the location of the SNCC Freedom House, where young organizers from all over the country stayed while working with local residents who were seeking the right to vote. Fittingly, the town of White Hall is the site of the Interpretive Center. (Years later, when I asked him how he got out of jail, Mayor Jackson told me that my daddy had gotten him out.)

When Black residents gathered to protest the unfair arrests, their demonstration was broken up by local white vigilantes. That evening, about forty Black people gathered at the home of a local family who were SNCC organizers. The meeting was underway when the house was ambushed by Klansmen, who fired guns into the home. There were rumors that Stokely Carmichael was inside and had been killed. The violence escalated to such an extent that a Montgomery National Guard unit was summoned. An SNCC news release reported, "At about 5 a.m. police ordered those in the house outside. Three SNCC workers were arrested for inciting a riot. SNCC reported that the Alabama State Patrol had 'taken over the town' and was searching people's homes. Forcing Black people on the street into their homes and denying entry to the town by persons from out of town. . . . At least three men were beaten by the police."

My mother's first cousins were in the house at the time of the attack, and one of them was shot by local law enforcement. When he'd visit our parents' house, we kids were fascinated to learn that he still had a bullet lodged in his head. The event became another searing point of reference for the community. For my family, it was not only of national significance but also personal.

I was just a child when the site where the Interpretive Center now sits was transformed from an open field into a massive tent city. The location was not far from the property my family would eventually own. To ensure that Black people would continue to be disenfranchised despite the Voting Rights Act, local landowners evicted sharecroppers who tried to register to vote. The white owners who kicked them off their land—land these families had lived on and worked since slavery—assumed this meant they would leave the county and take their votes with them. But for two years, SNCC activists and local leaders like my parents aided them in staying in the area by democratizing that site, bringing cots and tents and water and food, helping them find jobs and some stability. The site became known as Tent City. The support didn't just come from people from Lowndes, who were eager to help but were often too poor to assist financially; financial support also came from unions from as far as Detroit, with Black workers from the United Auto Workers, for instance, playing crucial roles. The UAW focused on workers' rights but also supported civil rights, despite their employers' attempts to undermine them.

Unions were very much a part of the Civil Rights Movement, especially in local struggles like those in Lowndes. People who were traveling the fifty-four miles from Selma to Montgomery on the trail would often use this tent city as a place for fellowship, a meal, and some rest before continuing their journey. All this was in service of making sure, for the first time in most of their lives, they would have the dignity of casting a ballot. That the majority-Black population—most of us, like my family, descendants of enslaved people—might have the nerve to assert their constitutional rights reinforced the county's reputation as "Bloody Lowndes."

After the Civil Rights Act of 1964 passed and the Voting Rights Act became law a year later, our community became one of the critical locations for the work of SNCC. My family's home in Montgomery and later in Lowndes County became one of the many stops along an intricate network of organizers, akin to the Underground Railroad. Meanwhile, the charismatic young field secretary Stokely Carmichael and others gravitated to Lowndes County. During the 1965 Selma to Montgomery march, the Lowndes County Freedom Party was formed to organize Black voters there. It took as its symbol the black panther. Get-out-the-vote posters of the time—geared also to illiterate voters who could easily understand the symbolism—posed the question, "Is this the party you want?" On the top of the poster was an illustration of a white rooster, chest thrust forward, with the banner "White Supremacy for the Right" surrounding it; the rooster was labeled as the "Democratic Party of Alabama," the segregationist party of Governor George Wallace. Then the question: "Or is this?" Below the rooster was a black panther, coiled and ready to pounce, representing "Lowndes County Freedom Organization." The final line: "One man—One vote."

The next year, Bobby Seale and Huey Newton took on the symbol and the name when they created the Black Panther Party in Oakland, California. Stokely Carmichael and other organizers discussed a get-out-the-vote strategy throughout Alabama, and a key element of that strategy was distributing the black-panther posters and leaflets, with both of my parents taking leading roles in advancing the movement.

I was a young child, but what I saw would stay with me for the rest of my life. I learned how important it was to have a goal, and that people working together for the common good can achieve transformative results. I also learned that patience was an essential ingredient: If something was worth fighting for, giving up was never an option.

This is the history that the Interpretive Center seeks to commemorate so that people never forget what happened in Bloody Lowndes. This is a safe place where visitors are encouraged to confront the past but also to use the opportunity to understand, or "interpret," its resonance today—both personally and within society as a whole. How much has changed? How much has remained the same? What would we do as individuals had we lived back then? I feel a special connection to this site not just because I'm deeply attached to the location and to what happened there. In 1997, I was the director of the National Voting Rights Museum in Selma when I traveled to Washington, DC, to attend the ceremony in the Old Executive Office Building that established the Interpretive Center. Years later, I was at the site in Lowndes County when ground was broken, and I returned again for its opening day, August 26, 2006.

Even though I had been part of the planning, I was awed when I saw the vast structure rise in the distance, a reimagined version of the Edmund Pettus Bridge. The large exhibition space spans an impressive 12,235 square feet. Its entrance is marked by two towering rectangular pillars that frame the doorway, also reminiscent of the entrance to the Sixteenth Street Baptist Church, where a bomb had been detonated in 1963, killing four young Black girls. Visitors enter its expansive interior and can go into one of two wings, each adorned with arched roofs that infuse each exhibition hall with diffuse light, almost as if there were little separation between inside and outside. Situated on the site of Tent City, the exhibition space now stands as a symbol of transformation and progress, a poignant juxtaposition of past and present.

Generations to come would learn about the contribution of Lowndes County residents in the fight for one of the most basic principles in democracy—the right to vote for a government representative of all people. There were multimedia exhibits, oral histories, photographs, and interviews with civil rights activists like Georgia Gilmore from Montgomery and Joanne Bland from Selma. I remembered activists Bob Mants, John Jackson, and Willie "Mukasa" Ricks from my childhood. A firm was hired to record and film many personal stories of the Selma to Montgomery march, as well as remembrances of the people of Lowndes County. When I took high school and college students to the Interpretive Center, the history came alive. They could walk through replicas of our county store and a tent that housed a family in Tent City.

On a much more practical level, the Interpretive Center was also a useful rest area since public bathrooms were not very common in this rural community. I have become an expert in sewage. We all have that need in common, and yet our access to sanitary, resilient, and sustainable waste management systems are, like so much in society, absurdly unequal. Years after the battle for civil rights in the 1960s, Lowndes County was where I embarked on my own battle for the human right of sanitation justice. The open sewage that many poor residents of my community had been forced to endure was a microcosm of a worldwide catastrophe. The clean, accessible restrooms at the center—despite also being connected to a failing septic system—are needed in this area, but they are also a symbol of the necessary work that remains to be done.

IT SEEMED ESPECIALLY FITTING that my community would once again call upon the 1964 Civil Rights Act—so crucial in beginning to turn the tide of systemic racism in Lowndes County—to address the public health crisis there. The sanitation needs of poor, rural, and Black and brown communities in all sixty-seven

Alabama counties had been ignored. Septic tanks are failing everywhere, and the misery of open sewage has plagued generations. A victory for the Black Belt could help all residents suffering the public health consequences of failing septic tanks no matter where they are located, their economic status, or their race.

Back in 2018 during the Trump administration, we worked with the organization Earthjustice to file our first complaint using Title VI of the Civil Rights Act. That section says that any program receiving federal funding—which included the Alabama Department of Public Health—cannot discriminate on the basis of race, color, or national origin. Our complaint alleged that the Alabama Department of Public Health and the Lowndes County Health Department had discriminated against Black residents of Lowndes County through their onsite wastewater-disposal program and infectious diseases and outbreaks program.

Our complaint outlined how Black residents were less likely to have access to functional septic systems, and how these agencies had failed to address the rampant raw-sewage problem, ignored and mischaracterized the evidence of hookworm in the county, and enforced criminal sanitation laws. These were especially egregious examples of another aspect of environmental injustice in which the very people who were too poor to have adequate sanitation were prosecuted by laws that literally criminalized lack of sanitation. Had these public institutions violated Title VI of the Civil Rights Act of 1964 by treating the Black residents in this community differently from others? Did the health department's policies and practices cause this population to have diminished access to adequate sanitation systems that made them vulnerable to disease and illness?

Naturally, I knew the answer to these questions. I had spent years trying to bring attention to the public health crisis in my community. I could show how people who lived there disproportionately and unjustifiably bore the risk of adverse health effects associated with inadequate wastewater treatment. One only needed to see how residents suffered from pervasive hookworm and other intestinal parasites, all transferred through fecal matter.

I didn't realize that my visit, in 2015, with a family who lived near a hole in the ground full of raw sewage, would be one of the first steps in creating a massive file of legal evidence. I had worn a dress and emerged from our meeting with my legs covered in mosquito bites. Then I developed a mysterious rash that no doctor seemed able to diagnose. I began to wonder if I was suffering from a condition common in underdeveloped regions, given that our citizens lived in comparable circumstances.

Around that time, I came across a *New York Times* op-ed written by Dr. Peter Hotez, a tropical and infectious disease specialist at Baylor College of Medicine in Houston. Dr. Hotez's research focused on how diseases once thought to have been eradicated were found in impoverished communities in wealthy countries. In the essay, "Tropical Diseases: The New Plague of Poverty," he described how the twenty million Americans living in extreme poverty, notably in Louisiana, Mississippi, and Alabama, now suffer from "a group of infections known as the neglected tropical diseases, which we ordinarily think of as confined to developing countries." Two of the major reasons for this, he wrote, were poor plumbing and sanitation. Could this be taking place in Lowndes County?

I wrote to him and told him about my experience in Lowndes County. It so happened he was attending a tropical-disease conference in Atlanta the following week, and he asked me to meet him there. He told me that he and his team wanted to conduct a study of residents in Lowndes County to see if they might be suffering from hookworm and other tropical parasites.

After a meticulous peer-reviewed study that took nearly three years, researchers found that 34.5 percent of the adults and children in the community tested positive for parasitic intestinal worms. Raw sewage was the likely culprit that led to hookworm and other diseases. We cited this study in our complaint, alleging that the Alabama Department of Public Health had failed to address the raw sewage on the ground, mischaracterized the hookworm study, and failed to investigate further. Furthermore, the department didn't even bother to keep sufficient data to comply with Title VI. Clearly, we had a case, but it would take time.

In 2021, under the Biden administration, we learned that an investigation based on our complaint would be conducted by the Civil Rights Division of the US Department of Justice and the US Department of Health and Human Services. What made this case historically significant was that it was the first time that Title VI had been used to investigate an environmental justice complaint. Once more, my community was in the position to tilt the arc of history.

And then, in May 2023, came another historic development: the DOJ and HHS reached an interim settlement with the Alabama Department of Public Health. It was the first time the DOJ had secured a resolution agreement in an environmental justice investigation under federal civil rights laws. In the agreement, the DOJ and HHS acknowledged that most Lowndes County residents do not have the means to obtain and maintain a state-permitted septic system. The agreement further stated that the Alabama Department of Public Health's operations "raise concerns about noncompliance with Title VI," including the state agency's enforcement of state criminal sanitation and property lien laws, as well as its failure to address the health risks associated with raw-sewage exposure for Black residents in Lowndes County.

I MOVED AWAY FROM my old hometown years ago and now live in northern Alabama, about a three-hour drive from Lowndes County, but I think I could probably do that drive in my sleep. So when I was asked to come for the announcement of these findings—a gathering that included DOJ and HHS representatives and officials, a US district attorney for Alabama, Earthjustice attorneys, and local residents—I wanted to be no place else. Fittingly, the landmark announcement would be held at the Interpretive Center.

It was a beautiful, early spring Alabama day, with the pale green shoots on trees and in meadows poised to burst forth. In Lowndes County, the red clay soil and the high water table are among the reasons why the septic systems and the infrastructure in these communities are damaged. Every time I return home, passing the property where I grew up, I am appalled by the ways our country forces people to live.

We started the day by bringing the government officials to visit two families in the county. I make it a point to take visitors into the poorest areas, where people live in mobile homes with no septic systems. I feel proud that I can bring officials, historians, activists, doctors, journalists, lawyers, and members of Congress to see what we are fighting for. Describing these circumstances, no matter how vividly, is nothing like seeing the dark liquid pools of human excrement, smelling the fetid air, looking at the modest mobile homes where families are raising children and coping with this mess day after day after day. I am part of this community; they are my cousins, my blood. Even those I am not biologically related to know my family. They trust me. Before I bring anyone to their homes, I make sure to get their consent. And for the most part, after having been ignored for generations, our residents are eager for the opportunity to have someone bear witness. I told our guests that these families also deserved to be mentioned in the Interpretive Center for having fought for the right to vote fifty years before, using the same legal mechanism we were using today to fight the sanitation crisis.

After the visit, we returned to the Interpretive Center. The group walked through the exhibit on the history of voting rights in Lowndes County. It added unforgettable context to their visit. But this day was different. The bleak circumstances they had witnessed were framed by the optimistic conviction that our actions, resulting in the day's historic announcement, would lead to meaningful change.

THE VISIT FROM THESE OFFICIALS had gone well; it was a beautiful day, full of hope and happiness and history. I told them I needed to leave because my drive back home would take three hours. We said our goodbyes, and before my COO and I left, I went to the ladies' room. A strong smell of disinfectant lingered in the air. The roll of toilet paper was so tightly wound I figured that it must have been purchased at the local Dollar General. I knew I'd end up shredding what felt like half the roll, just to get it in shape to be used—and by that time wouldn't it have been worth buying a slightly more expensive brand?

And then, suddenly, everything changed—the glow of the day, the victorious feeling of having made momentous strides. Even the absurdity of the toilet paper. The energy in the room shifted. The ions in the room had become charged with a kind of danger that I didn't understand but only perceived instinctively.

I looked up and saw a tall man peering down over the stall. His eyes looked glazed—something was off. In one move I stood and pulled up my underwear and pants and told him, in a calm but commanding voice, that he needed to leave. I was frightened but tried to summon authority. He began to push the door of the stall, violently, insistently, and that was when my calm facade completely crumbled.

I've had dreams where I am in danger and unable to call for help. Where I'm under serious threat, and somehow whatever cry might save me is lodged in the back of my throat, unable to escape. It's a terrible feeling of paralysis and powerlessness and rising panic. But in real life, at that moment, I found my voice.

I started to scream, worrying that I wouldn't be heard through the concrete walls and down the hall. I screamed and screamed as this man slammed his body repeatedly against the door. The door was all that stood between me and his frenzy. Desperately, I hoped someone would appear and stop him. Even in my terror, questions ricocheted in my mind: Could anyone hear me? Who was this man? A stranger who had randomly stopped by the Interpretive Center? A local? Why was he in the women's bathroom? Had he been following me? What was his intent? And why didn't my screams make him stop?

There were law enforcement officials who were part of our group, but clearly no one could hear me. This was not supposed to happen here. I was home. I was at the Interpretive Center. I was in danger, convinced I was fighting for my life. I screamed so loudly that my voice began to crack and my throat was shredded with pain. We were locked in a struggle. Tears were running down my face as I pushed against the door.

Events seemed to be unfolding outside of time, in a strange slow motion. I learned later that this sensation is in fact a kind of coping mechanism, shared by most people in the midst of traumatic events. In order to give ourselves time to come up with protective reactions to the danger, our brains actually break down the traumatic event so we experience it in a slower way.

Only the flimsiest lock seals a restroom stall. It manages to keep the door closed but can hardly withstand the strength of a powerful man determined to break it down. I was terrified to contemplate what would happen if he got inside. I would be trapped in this small space. I would have been easily overpowered. I pushed with all my might to keep the door closed. Then there was the briefest of pauses. Had he left?

Suddenly, a hand gripped my ankle. He'd gone to the side of the stall, reached under, and grabbed my leg. It was like a horror movie. The physical contact was even more terrifying as I kicked and squirmed and loosened his grip. My screams grew louder and more desperate, my voice hoarse. Where was everyone?

I have no idea how much time actually passed, but just as suddenly, he left. I didn't realize the danger had passed until I heard the voices of two women asking if I was okay. They assured me that he was gone. I left the stall, shaking and afraid. My throat was on fire. I can't remember if I said anything to the women. I didn't rinse the tears off my face. I just wanted—I *needed*—to get as far away from that space as fast as I could.

THE COO OF MY ORGANIZATION, with whom I had traveled to the event, had stopped the young man as he emerged from the ladies' room and prevented him from leaving until he was certain that I wasn't harmed.

"Are you okay, Catherine?" he asked, worry etched on his face.

"Yes, yes, I'm okay," I responded, still shaking and unsure if I was telling the truth. "Get me out of here."

I could stand, though my legs were weak. My throat felt as if I'd been choked. I felt nauseated. I was not harmed physically— but I was traumatized.

My mind shattered into a million pieces. I was a victim. I was a member of the community. I was an advocate. I was a Black woman who had been attacked, as Black women are attacked hundreds of times every day. I was an integral part of a historic day in the environmental justice movement. I was a leader. I was vulnerable. I was a mother. I was the daughter of two heroes of the Civil Rights Movement. I was responsible for my community. I was a Christian. I was home in Lowndes County. I did not feel safe.

This is what trauma looks like: first, events unfold in slow motion; then when the danger is past and the body floods with adrenaline, one's mind begins to race, taking in all the details at a speed that bears no resemblance to the external world. Even as I briefly tried to compose myself in the hall, I looked more closely at the young man my COO was preventing from leaving. The knot in my stomach tightened. I knew this young man. I knew his family. Their activism had contributed to the moment we were commemorating today. They too had been victims of sewage inequality. I had seen him walk into the meeting, but I hadn't recognized him earlier. I only recognized him now because he was there with his grandparents.

The people from the Interpretive Center were concerned, bombarding me with questions. Should they call the sheriff? Did I want to press charges? Was I all right? Did I need medical attention? They were shocked and horrified and sorry. Something like this had never happened at the center. How horrible for it to happen at all and to happen to me. Was there anything that they could do for me? Did I need to sit down? Have a glass of water? They urged me to file a report with the sheriff. But all I knew at that moment was that I just needed to get out of that place.

I looked at my assailant, a young Black man who was clearly unwell. My mind scattered in wildly associative directions all at once. I thought about the Central Park Five—wrongly convicted and demonized because they were guilty of being young Black men. That was all it took to ruin their lives. Why is it that white assailants who go into schools and kill children are instantly deemed "mentally unstable"? No such luxury is afforded Black men. I thought of Matthew Reeves, a young Black man who had a profound intellectual disability, with an IQ score in the sixties. Alabama nevertheless put him to death for having robbed a man of $360 before killing him. Reeves was so impaired he was unable to choose the method of his own execution. The case went all the way to the Supreme Court, who, in a 5–4 decision, permitted the state to execute him.

The young man before me was not innocent. I knew this. But could I allow his assault on me to overtake the story of this sacred site, to demonize his family, to overshadow the progress we had made to address the injustices against the residents of Lowndes County? My attacker was likely mentally ill. I reflected on my Christian upbringing. I found within me compassion. And I also thought about how I wanted this day to be remembered.

I needed to process what had happened, on a day that should have been spent celebrating a momentous achievement. Over the years, we have seen the Civil Rights Act and the Voting Rights Act undermined in our courts and in our politics. But we had attempted something audacious—linking environmental justice with civil rights—and we had succeeded. That was what mattered on May 4, 2023. I knew that if I pressed charges, if a sheriff appeared, if the young man was taken into custody, the media would soon get hold of the story. And a story about an assault in a public restroom at the Lowndes County Interpretive Center would eclipse the far more consequential and lasting story, one that was the culmination of years of work and made newly relevant a piece of legislation that was nearly sixty years old.

And yet in that moment I felt so completely alone. There was no one to whom I could turn to help unpack the cascading thoughts coursing through my head and my heart. I knew that deciding what the next steps would be depended entirely on me. It was becoming clear, despite the tumult: I would swallow my pain that day. I could do nothing to diminish or undermine the victory for the residents of my county. Even though it was possible this young man might repeat this kind of assault. My concern that he get the mental health care that he so clearly needed outweighed any impulse to seek resolution in a court of law.

It all felt so surreal; I just needed to leave. The workers there tried to get me to remain, but I was forceful and clear. I told my COO that we needed to get going. We got in the car and drove in silence. I stared out the window.

As a Black woman, with brothers and a daughter and two grandchildren, with family tragedies in my past, I was not under any illusion about the perils of the world. But even so, the world felt markedly less safe after that day. I never travel alone, and now, whenever I need to use a restroom in a public space—an airport, say, or a university where I am speaking—I have a companion with me. My body holds the tension and the fear in these spaces. Like a phantom limb, I felt his hand grabbing my leg for days afterward. And there were so many what-ifs. What if he had broken in? What if I had pressed charges? What if I had been physically injured?

When the immediacy of the trauma had receded a bit, I called an old friend, Bryan Stevenson, a criminal justice activist, legal scholar, and visionary. We had worked together at his organization, the Equal Justice Initiative, in Montgomery and had become close friends. Bryan's entire career as a public-interest lawyer has focused on offering substantive help and representation for members of communities who rarely received this kind of support: incarcerated people, poor people, and people on death row. If anyone could advise me in this situation, it would be him.

Bryan urged me to speak to the sheriff and supported my decision not to press charges. Instead, he encouraged me to urge the sheriff to seek mental health counseling for this young man. I followed his advice and spoke to the sheriff and his investigators, and I filed a report with the understanding that they would request a mental health evaluation of the young man.

Several months later, I received a call from one of the investigators saying that the perpetrator had admitted to the offense, but they would not seek a mental health evaluation. I felt a profound disappointment, even as I was not surprised. The sheriff is a Black man, someone I know well, and the investigators were all white. What was playing out before me was yet another expression of deeply embedded racism and classism in the criminal justice system. Because this young, poor Black man had admitted his transgression, law enforcement deemed him mentally fit. "Nothing was wrong with him," one investigator said. "He knew exactly what he was doing and should go to prison." They asked me to press charges and seek a warrant for his arrest. I didn't have to give it much thought. This young man, like so many others who find themselves in trouble with the law, needed mental health care, not incarceration. The fact that no one would make this kind of an effort saddened me. I declined to file charges against him, which was the only option that I was given. That was the last time I spoke to the investigators about the case.

ARRIVING AT MY DECISION, however, did not erase how traumatized I was by the event. But the climate in this country does not allow me to be vulnerable. I have learned to remain strong and grieve for my losses through action. I stay focused on righteousness, equality, and the generations to come. And I have been sustained, as my enslaved ancestors were, as my parents were, as civil rights workers the world over have been, by my love of God.

In the world of activism, we often must sacrifice our personal concerns for the higher good. I saw that in my parents, in the people memorialized in the Interpretive Center, in the faces of our friends and family members who fought to make the world better for me, my daughter, and my grandchildren.

And I know that our work is continuing to make the world a better place.

After our complaint was filed, the Civil Rights Division of the DOJ and HHS found that Alabama officials knew that Black residents in Lowndes County were suffering from failing septic systems and did nothing to stop it. When Assistant Attorney General Kristen Clarke, who had been with us that day at the Interpretive Center, announced the decision, she said, "Today starts a new chapter for Black residents of Lowndes County, Alabama, who have endured health dangers, indignities, and racial injustice for far too long."

The Alabama Department of Public Health is now required to provide basic sanitation services and stop punishing poor people unable to afford to upgrade their failing systems. In October 2023, we filed another complaint against the Alabama Department of Environmental Management. This time, we worked with the National Resources Defense Council and the Southern Poverty Law Center to persuade the EPA's Office of Environmental Justice and External Civil Rights to open a broad investigation of the Clean Water State Revolving Fund. I hope the federal investigation will result in positive change for any Alabama resident currently relying on a failing onsite sanitation system and for all US communities for whom justice is long overdue.

As for the young man whose grandparents I knew, they never reached out to me personally. I don't blame them. What do you say in a situation like this? I haven't reached out to them either. There is too much pain on both sides. I truly don't know what more I could have done. Someday, I know we will run into each other in Lowndes County. We'll smile and start a careful conversation because I still have deep affection for that family. We'll remember that day and how I hugged his grandmother before I went to the restroom. And we will do our best to move forward.

So, yes—change is happening. Our eyes are on the prize, as the old Gospel hymn goes, but often our bodies and our souls are wounded in the process. We learn to ignore our own suffering and persevere with patience and determination to achieve a just end. Even in victory, one must smile like a beauty queen onstage, brushing off the tears, heartbreak, and disappointment as we move forward on our path. I am not a saint, but love sustains me—for my people, my country, my planet, and my Redeemer. Love makes it possible for me to contain my pain. I rejoice in the progress we make and the progress yet to come.

TEN

I Am the Answer
to My Ancestors' Prayers

MATTIE COLEMAN, MY MOTHER, WAS SIXTY-TWO YEARS OLD when she was murdered. No one in our community could have foreseen that her life would have ended in such a way. She was one of those essential women, the kind of person who could be relied upon to solve the problems that made others throw up their hands in despair. She didn't call attention to herself, but people sought her out because she lived her faith through service. Providing to others was as natural as the beating of her heart.

My father's death two years earlier was crushing for her. Theirs was a beautiful, old-fashioned marriage, devoted and loving, a partnership in which one could finish the other's sentence. When my mother inhaled, my father exhaled the same breath. When my father passed, she grieved in ways that were both public and private, but she was not broken by the loss as so many others might have been. She found solace in her faith. She carried on. She organized her life around his absence, doing what she had always done—filling the empty space with family and friends and with people who needed her. And people always seemed to need her.

The man who murdered my mother was no stranger; he was in fact a distant family member, because everyone in Lowndes County, it seems, is either connected by blood or marriage. In the simplest rendition of events, this is what happened: A wheelchair-bound man, who also had emotional issues and was receiving mental health care, turned to my mother for help, and of course she responded. She took him to his appointments, and his family would ask her to talk to him whenever he was agitated, and she obliged, an essential calming presence. Who could blame him for asking for help again and again and again? She was someone he relied on, but his dependence became unsettling to her. One day, in December 2002, he had a headache. Even though she had tried to distance herself, when he asked her to pick up some medication for him at the drugstore, she did. They were in his bedroom when he took her life. And then he killed himself.

I have no words to describe my grief. I was my mother's first child and her confidante, and she was mine. From the time I was a preteen throughout my adulthood, she and I would talk most days, no matter where I was in the world. We would pick up just where we'd left off, easily wandering through subjects like current events, family, work, and relationships. When troubles entered my life, as they always did, she was the person I would call. When it was time for me to end a marriage—never having enjoyed the forever-love that she and my father had shared—I would shed my tears over the phone and know that when I hung up, I would feel so much better.

She had told me about him on our calls too. His mental health care workers had become alarmed by the way he had spoken about their relationship. She was no longer a friend who offered him support but someone who had become the focus of his obsession. He spoke about her constantly. He imagined that his feelings were reciprocated and that someday they would share a life together. His delusions were unsettling, and while she didn't express any fear, she thought it best to pull back. I agreed and believed that the situation could be controlled. After all, they were in Lowndes County, where people looked after each other.

I know that my mother was seeing someone at the time, and that felt reassuring to me. But she also told me that in the fevered imaginings of the wheelchair-bound man's unsettled mind, jealousy had started to appear. He didn't want her to be with anyone if it was not going to be him. "I think I just need to back off," she said. "I hate to hurt him, but I know that he has other family and support." I encouraged her to act and reflected on that conversation hundreds of times.

Even if she had died peacefully in bed at ninety-nine years old, I would have felt that she had passed too soon. But the brutality of her death was almost too much to bear. I am painfully aware of the terrible statistics about the killing of Black women: that they are murdered with more than six times the frequency of their white counterparts and more than any other demographic. The method is most often firearms. I knew all this intellectually and had tremendous sympathy for all the Black mothers and daughters and sisters and friends whose lives have been senselessly lost. But these statistics never seem personally relevant, never rock your world to its foundations, until your mother becomes one of them.

In the midst of that vast landscape of suffering, even when the worst thing that could possibly have taken place had occurred, I tried to find moments of comfort in Scripture. As Paul wrote to the Philippians in 4:6–7, "Do not be anxious about anything, but in every situation, by prayer and petition, with thanksgiving, present your requests to God. And the peace of God, which transcends all understanding, will guard your hearts and your minds in Christ Jesus." I tried to believe this. I craved that "peace of God." I needed to believe it was possible. But the event had a seismic impact on my life, ripping it in two: the decades of peace and comfort when I had a mother, and the decades of loneliness and loss after her passing. And that peace from Scripture seemed a blessed gift from a distant past.

I was living in Montgomery when I received the call from one of my brothers with the catastrophic news that my mom had been shot. What I did not know was whether she was still alive. I felt a chill and then a numbness as I waited for word of her well-being. I missed a call from the sheriff, and when I called him back, he told me that she was gone. My brother called moments later, but by that time, I already knew. "How could this have happened?" I asked repeatedly. I knew this was a question no one could answer at that point, not just because answers were not available, but because anyone I turned to was as crushed and distraught by the news as I was. Somehow, I found myself surrounded by my cousins and a few of my oldest, dearest friends, who miraculously appeared at my house to try to offer some comfort and support, but all I knew was that I had to get to Lowndes County that night.

They knew I couldn't travel back home alone, so they accompanied me. There were three carloads of us.

As soon as we arrived in Lowndes County, we went to our family home, where my mother's nieces and nephews and some more of my dear friends had come together. I thought of the delight my mother would have felt to have our home filled with so many people who loved our family and especially loved her—but now the beating heart of that residence had been brutally stopped. The woman who had made it a home, whose garden was fallow in the winter but would have been overflowing with produce come summer, was now lying in our local funeral home, waiting for us. In the kitchen cupboards were the mason jars of fruit given to her by relatives and people in the community who still canned their own food. She had long stopped this practice because her children were no longer at home. Her precious hats were all in their right places. Everything was the same and would never be the same again.

I was driven to the funeral home by my friends, where I met the rest of my family. Her memorial service would be the following day, and this would be our opportunity for a moment with her. I couldn't remember the last time I'd eaten. My entire body felt tied in knots. I felt physically bound by grief and the surreal knowledge that viewing her lifeless body would force me to acknowledge what I dreaded having to accept. It was one thing to know; it was another thing to see. She was gone from this life. I was without a mother and a father, orphaned.

We entered the funeral home where we had mourned the passing of so many others, but this time was different. The owner, whom we had known for years, greeted us with the quiet compassion that was part of his profession, but there was something else there. He was grieving too. He ushered us into the small room where she lay, and, as the oldest child, I entered first, supported by my brothers. Taking a deep breath, I hesitated before looking at her through my tears, and then I let my eyes rest on that beloved face. I saw no pain, no suffering, only her gentle smile and the dimples her children had inherited.

And the peace of God, which surpasses all understanding, will guard your hearts and your minds in Christ Jesus.

Until that moment, I never thought I would be capable of smiling again. But seeing her, I returned her gentle smile with my own. The expression on her face made it easier for me to take the first few steps on the journey of living the rest of my life without her. It didn't change the fact that my mother was gone. It didn't change the fact that I would suffer in my grief and be ambushed by sorrow. It was the most difficult period of my life. But within that vast wilderness, God offered me respite and peace. I felt his tender mercies.

The following day was the funeral, and we gathered once again at my parents' house, now crowded with relatives from both sides of the family. Her young granddaughters each wore one of her hats in her memory. We left our last childhood home and made our way to the Central High School gym in Lowndes County, where we held the celebration of her life. No church would be big enough. Sarah, a longtime friend whose family owned the funeral home, was in the car with us. "Look behind us," she said. I looked through the rear window and saw cars lined up in the funeral procession as far as the eye could see. More than two thousand people attended her service. Nearly as many men as women were there, an unusual occurrence and similar in size and makeup to the crowd that had attended my father's service.

The cars pulled up to the school, and then it was time for us to enter. As we walked down the center aisle, everyone stood, making a loud whooshing sound like a great breath of air. Slowly I walked with my brothers and sister, escorted by my old friends Vesper Osborne and Sheila Frazier. People I hadn't seen in years had come from out of town. Classmates with whom I'd walked these halls in high school were present, joined in shock and grief. Every year of my life was represented by the people in that gym, everywhere I had lived—Detroit; Washington, DC; Los Angeles; and all over the South. People sat in chairs and on the bleachers; others stood on the side of the room and in the back, wherever they could find a spot.

My mother loved music, and we made sure that this celebration would be filled with it. Many of our musically gifted friends had asked if they could pay their respects by performing. My mother was not a sad person, and as heartbreaking as this occasion was, we wanted the music to lift up our broken spirits. Ministers in the community were eager to lead the service, but my brother Jay C, a minister himself, would preach. I worried his grief might get the better of him, but the words he spoke and the memories he shared had two thousand people smiling and nodding and crying and celebrating Mattie Coleman in the way she deserved. He succeeded in doing the impossible: he replaced the horror of her death with the glories of the way she lived.

Of all the music performed that day, one moment stood out. A tremendously talented group of singers called the Cobb Sisters sang "The Battle Is Not Yours," the song that Yolanda Adams had made her own. The refrain became a kind of prayer for me during those dark days:

> No matter what you're going through
> Remember God is using You
> For the battle is not yours, it's the Lord's

Martin Luther King III sent a letter that was read at the service. I had first met him when I served as an intern at the King Center in Atlanta. We were the same age and became fast friends. Now we had a different, painful point of solidarity. My mother, a crusader for faith and justice and civil rights, had been gunned down. My Black family too had joined the ranks of those who had lost a loved one to gun violence.

Nothing in my life had prepared me for the misery of those days around my mother's death. Yet my life had prepared me in a different way. That time was filled with more love and support that I have ever experienced, and that strengthened me in ways I only now fully appreciate. These friends and family also gave me the reason to carry on with my work. At that low point, I might have been tempted to give up my activism. So much had been taken from me that I could easily conclude I had nothing left to give. But the fact that so many people embraced us and celebrated my mother's life and the Coleman family showed me there is nothing I would rather do than work for these people, who had shown us all so much love through the years. No matter which stairs I climb, I'm always going to be from Lowndes County. My mother's death taught me an enduring lesson: In the darkest of times, hope is still possible. Indeed, it is essential.

AS EVERYONE WHO HAS ENDURED grief and trauma knows, time helps. The fierce anguish of loss is replaced with a different intensity; the all-consuming self-immolation at the beginning gives way to grief as a constant companion, an ache in the heart, a phantom limb. Then every once in a while, one is ambushed by loss again. It may not last as long or be experienced as intensely as it was during those early months, but the pain is still shockingly acute, and then it subsides.

My mother understood these kinds of feelings after my father died. She grieved powerfully. She loved him with all her heart. And one way she found comfort in the midst of her loss was through her faith. My mother grew up in the Bethesda Missionary Baptist Church, a denomination of the Baptist Church that emerged as part of the Second Great Awakening in the first part of the nineteenth century, in which members are committed to the need for "missionary" work—preaching and evangelizing the word of the Lord to all parts of the world.

One of the great historical figures in this tradition was Lott Carey, a once-enslaved preacher who managed to buy his freedom from his owners in Virginia in 1813. Lott Carey was determined to spread the gospel throughout the world, especially to Africa. In 1821, with remarkable bravery, he took several fellow Black missionaries on the reverse journey of most of their peers, who had come in shackles. This group returned to Africa as free men, determined to set up churches and schools. Using Liberia as his home base, he created the First Baptist Church of Liberia, where he also established schools and health care for the community.

Lott Carey died in 1828, but the legacy he created has endured to this day in the tradition of missionary work in these countries. To this day there is an organization in his honor, the Lott Carey Foreign Missions Society, which was founded in 1897 and continues to provide churches and schools and health care for communities in Liberia and other places in Africa.

I often thought that both of my parents should have been preachers; many people thought that my father was, with his beautiful voice and commanding dignity. They were both so proud when my brother Jay C became a minister, as if his vocation satisfied one of their secret hopes. My mother could have served as a minister as well, though this was yet another option that was completely closed off for women of her generation. They could have been ministers' *wives*, of course, or leaders of the church ladies, or they maybe even could have assumed prominent roles in their choirs—though I can't remember a woman choir director when I was growing up. But to stand in front of the congregation and preach? Impossible.

Instead, my mother performed her missionary work as a Missionary Baptist not from the pulpit nor by going on trips to far corners of the world. Her missionary work was caring for those in Lowndes County, healing and helping and being a living example of a Christian life. And in my own life, I suppose I too have internalized the messages of the incalculable number of Sunday mornings at church with her. I spread the gospel of racial justice. Like my mother, I try to speak for the poor and the vulnerable. We both have attempted to do what Jesus urged in Matthew 25:40: "Whatever you did for one of the least of these brothers and sisters of mine, you did for me."

This was the central theme of my mother's missionary work. I have found that in my faith and in the inspiration I receive from the Lord, I feel her presence as she accompanies me every day, every hour, wherever I travel in the world. As we sang during her service,

> *No matter what you're going through*
> *Remember God is using You*
> *For the battle is not yours, it's the Lord's*

WHEN I SPEAK TO AUDIENCES, whether they're made up of older folks or college or high school students, invariably, they come up to me afterward with a request. "The world around us is so bleak," they say. "Please, Catherine, give us some reason not to despair."

There are so many reasons to feel hopeful, I reply. Look at the leadership young people are displaying in order to build a more resilient society that can survive climate change. I feel hope when I see them fighting the righteous fight to keep the planet healthy, so that Earth will be livable for generations to come. I point to the way that people are incorporating Indigenous wisdom as we try to roll back those systems that have created the inequities we are suffering. Indigenous people always understood that water is life and should be infused with its spiritual power and not treated as a mere commodity.

I look at how we are all connecting with our ancestors through science and DNA. After the burdens of our history of racial terror, there is great promise in discovering where we are from and how we are all interconnected. Another place I turn to and see

vast reasons for hope is in the HBCUs, which have not only survived but are thriving, with unprecedented numbers of brilliant
young students choosing to attend them over Ivy League institutions. The enormous growth and prosperity of so many Black
people—a visible and vibrant Black middle class—and the commitment of this community to share their time and treasures, this
gives me hope.

I feel hope when I look at the new Poor People's Campaign,
as it persistently and heroically raises up people who have been
ignored and marginalized. I am inspired by those who are fighting the righteous fight to keep our democracy healthy, so we have
a country filled with vast possibilities instead of cruel constraints.

I feel hope when I look at all the families who have lost loved
ones to gun violence. The families from Columbine, from Sandy
Hook, the young people from Marjory Stoneman Douglas High
School, from Emanuel Church in Charleston and the Tree of Life
Synagogue in Pittsburgh—this community of advocates for gun
control and of righteous people who practice the power of forgiveness. At the arraignment of the gunman in Charleston, two
days after the horrific mass shooting in Emanuel Church, families of victims appeared to face Dylann Roof—the young white
man responsible for the massacre. "I forgive you," the daughter
of one of the victims said, setting the tone for what was repeated
throughout the hearing. Still coping with the deaths of their loved
ones, each person who spoke expressed forgiveness. As I read
about their holiness, their grace, their soaring faith, I wondered
if I too would have been capable of this when facing my mother's
murderer. I pray that I could have been. Perhaps if I had been

given the opportunity, I would have felt that amazing grace, and it would have made this possible.

A different kind of hope can emerge from these tragedies, not from forgiveness but from a different kind of justice. In the spring of 2023, in Nashville, Tennessee, three nine-year-old children and three adults at the Covenant School were murdered by a twenty-eight-year-old gunman, armed with an AR-15. The pattern following the tragedy was depressingly familiar: images of horrified parents, traumatized children, balloons and flowers and notes and teddy bears piled up in a deserted school playground, and politicians spouting bromides about mental health and the need for tougher consequences and better locks on school doors and on and on without ever coping with the essential problem.

But this time there was a slight variation. The attack took place on March 27, and three days later thousands of demonstrators appeared at the statehouse in Nashville to demand that the Tennessee General Assembly, dominated by gun-loyal Republicans, pass stricter gun laws after they had spent years loosening them. In 2021, Tennessee lawmakers passed a measure making permits optional for handguns and, weeks before the shooting, some GOP representatives were championing legislation to expand permitless open-carry laws to include long guns.

Among the demonstrators were two young Black lawmakers, Representatives Justin Jones and Justin Pearson—"the two Justins," as they came to be known—and a white woman, Representative Gloria Johnson. They not only participated in the gun-control protest but begged their Republican colleagues to pass more gun-law reforms. Instead, House Speaker Cameron

Sexton vowed that the representatives would face "conse-quences." Another representative who sponsored the resolution to expel them described their protests against gun violence, their outrage at more senseless slaughter, as a mere "temper tantrum." And how does the white patriarchy respond to uppity Black people? They punish them, of course. Whips and chains no lon-ger being an option, two days later they voted to expel the two Justins. They explained that expelling two Black men and not Representative Johnson was not about racism but only, they said, because her transgressions did not rise to the level of what they had done.

And now for the ray of hope in the midst of all this grief and despair: Pearson refused to go meekly into retirement. "Is what's happening outside these doors by Tennesseans who want to see change a 'temper tantrum'?" he said.

I was riveted by this drama, not just because it laid bare the breathtaking racism and cynicism of Republican lawmakers in Tennessee. Justin Pearson came into prominence as one of those idealistic young people fighting for climate justice. He and I have worked together since 2021, when he was leading the fight against the Byhalia Connection Pipeline that was supposed to transport fuel through his predominantly Black neighborhood in southwest Memphis to the Gulf of Mexico. Pearson realized that beneath the land the pipeline would be passing through was an aquifer sup-plying drinking water to more than a million people. I was intro-duced to Justin by a mutual climate-activist friend.

I was very impressed by the focus and the clarity of this young man—just twenty-six years old. The person who introduced us said that he reminded him of a young Dr. King. We spoke about community organizing and the flagrant example of environmental injustice this pipeline represented. We would call and check in with each other from time to time, and on Earth Day of that year, we did a virtual talk together at Ebenezer Baptist Church.

I felt such great hope in the two Justins' courageous acts. And yet, as the events in Tennessee unfolded, despair began to creep in. I felt we had gone back a couple of decades, when African Americans were not welcome in positions of power and, once again, those who were in power made no effort to hide their contempt. A fact that was even more galling because these young African American men were supporting mostly white mothers who were protesting for change. The two Justins had been ostracized for standing up for white children who had been murdered in school. It made me wonder: Did these so-called God-fearing Republicans have hearts at all? We know they have no consciences. I will never understand how American evangelical Christians are among the most passionate gun owners. A Pew study revealed that 41 percent of white evangelicals own a gun, compared with 30 percent of others in the US.

And yet again, my despair gave way to hope. Days after they had been expelled, the condemnation of the act was so universal that the two Justins were reinstated by local officials. And then, in June during the democratic primaries, both men won resounding victories.

As a Christian, I know that forgiveness is a central tenet of my faith and that redemption is available to everyone. As a parent, I also know that actions must have consequences. But even people whose names were synonymous with bigotry can change. And few names in Alabama were more synonymous with bigotry than that of Governor George Wallace, who famously cried during his 1963 inaugural address, "Segregation now. Segregation tomorrow. And segregation forever." While his four terms as governor coincided with the triumph of the Civil Rights Movement, he did all that he could to sabotage those triumphs in Alabama and secure his promise. Was there anyone in a position of power more committed to the oppression of Black people than he?

And yet even George Wallace could repent. In 1995, at the age of seventy-five, almost four years before his death and wheelchair-bound from a thwarted assassination attempt, he embarked on a failed run for a fifth term as governor. He met about two hundred civil rights marchers at the St. Jude Educational Institute in Montgomery who were commemorating the thirtieth anniversary of the Selma to Montgomery voting-rights march. His voice was weak and his hearing had abandoned him, but through an aide he apologized to them. "Those were different days, and we all in our own ways were different people. We have learned hard and important lessons in the thirty years that have passed between us since the days surrounding your first walk along Highway 80," the aide read. "Much has transpired since those days. A great deal has been lost and a great deal has been gained, and here we are. My message to you today is, Welcome to Montgomery. May your message be heard. May your lessons never be forgotten. May our history be always remembered."

Some of the marchers applauded; for others, the memories of his vile behavior and the damage he inflicted could never be forgotten. I counted myself at the time among the latter group. This kind of transformation seemed unlikely at best. And yet elders in our Lowndes County community had a different perspective, one deepened by history and experience. My parents described Wallace as Saul, a persecutor of Christians, being changed to Paul while he was on the road to Damascus. The young Catherine Coleman Flowers bristled at what I considered a kind of weakness or amnesia. But back then, I too was wrong, somehow overlooking the message of Jesus. How could we not celebrate the work of the Spirit in the miracle of repentance and transformation, when someone like Governor George Wallace was capable of seeing the errors of his ways? Maybe there is hope for others.

And there is the hope that I live, every single day, as a Black woman who was characterized as disadvantaged and marginalized, while growing up in a community that was disadvantaged and marginalized. And now I am able to walk among world leaders. And I am among them not as an affirmative action poster child but as a leader in my own right.

Most of all, I am hopeful because of my faith. Since childhood we have been taught that God acts in mysterious ways. When we pray, God hears us. He may say no, but he has listened to our entreaties. I lift my voice and sing his praise. He is with me and with all of us as we mark our days in this world. My parents, grandparents, and ancestors all over the globe accompany me as well. There are times when I look up and feel their presence, as close as if they were sitting at my kitchen counter. I cannot explain why, but I know the truth of it.

My daughter and grandchildren are the physical embodiment of a bright future, as are children all over the world. But they are also the spiritual and physical embodiment of our ancestors' prayers for Black children to grow up in a world where they are no longer relegated to the margins of society. And for me, that is the wellspring of hope forevermore.

So, yes, when I am asked how it is possible to still be hopeful, I am grateful for the question. It's been over twenty years since my mother's death. There is not a day that passes when I don't think about her. Sometimes, I remember her voice on the telephone. Other days, I think of her sitting in the front of our house, chatting with a neighbor. Or laughing with my father as we all sat around our kitchen table at the end of a long and happy dinner together, where we relished her sweet potato pie, ham, and greens from her garden. I see her bent over her sewing machine, working on a dress for one of us, or modeling a new hat, one that she was impatient to wear to church. Or hugging my daughter goodbye after a visit together.

Whenever I enjoy some success, I always feel a pang of regret that neither my mother nor my father are here to witness it. They didn't live long enough to see me become a homeowner. They never saw me win awards or have recognition for my work. Or publish a book. Or be invited to the White House to testify before Congress. Or trade stories about grandchildren with the president of the United States.

They never saw me win the MacArthur "Genius" Award. I wonder if they might have teased me just a little bit, proud as they would have been, for being called a "genius." "My daughter, the genius," I can hear my mother say, with pride but also with humor, to make sure that I didn't let this honor make me feel more important than I was.

When they died, my life was taking shape, but it was not close to what it would become. It would have been so much more meaningful for me if they had been there to smile and share in a success that never would have been possible without them— without their encouragement, their examples, and their prayers. And yet I believe, with complete conviction, that one reason I have had these blessings over the past two decades is because they are there on the other side, guiding me on my path.

I know that I am living out the dreams of my father and my mother. They passed the torch to me, and, at some point, I will pass that torch to my daughter and my grandchildren. When the time comes, I imagine that I will guide them from the other side, as the circle of life and redemption remains unbroken. Every day new answers arise, and when they do, the great blessing of a miracle called hope is like the loaves and fishes Jesus shared with the hungry crowd: the bounty only multiplies and sustains multitudes.

Notes

1. THIRTY PIECES OF SILVER

5. "But Jesus asked him, 'Judas, are you betraying the Son of Man with a kiss?'": Luke 22:48 (New International Version).

6. "The Son of Man will go just as it is written about him. But woe to that man who betrays the Son of Man! It would be better for him if he had not been born": Matt. 26:24 (New International Version).

7. more than a billion dollars have been spent influencing federal elections since the 2010 *Citizens United* case: Lee, Chisun, Douglas Keith, Katherine Valde, Benjamin T. Brickner, Ian Vandewalker, Lawrence Norden, Daniel I. Weiner, et al. "Dark Money." Brennan Center for Justice, June 26, 2016. https://www.brennancenter.org/issues/reform-money-politics/influence-big-money/dark-money.

10. There have been more than two thousand school shootings since Columbine: Riedman, David. "K-12 School Shooting Database." K-12 School Shooting Database. Accessed May 29, 2024. https://k12ssdb.org/.

10. In 2023 alone, there were nearly 350 school shootings across the country: Modan, Naaz, and Kara Arundel. "Another Record High: Counting School Shootings in 2023." K-12 DIVE, December 20, 2023. https://www.k12dive.com/news/2023-total-school-mass-shootings/703007/.

12. Compared with Germany, the United States has seventy-seven times the rate of homicides with guns; compared with France, we have 17 percent more gun-related deaths and compared with Australia, we have thirty-three times the rate of gun-related deaths: Leach-Kemon, Katherine, Rebecca Sirull, and Scott Glenn. "On Gun Violence, the United States Is an Outlier." Institute for Health Metrics and Evaluation (IHME), October 31, 2023. https://www.healthdata.org/news-events/insights-blog/acting-data/gun -violence-united-states-outlier.

12. At least twenty mass shootings have killed more than two hundred people in the state over the past sixty years: Priest, Jessica, and Perla Trevizo. "Despite Decades of Mass Shootings in Texas, Legislators Have Failed to Pass Meaningful Gun Control Laws." *Texas Tribune*, February 16, 2023. https:// www.texastribune.org/2023/02/16/mass-shootings-texas-gun-control/.

12. The year of the Uvalde massacre, the NRA poured more than $5 million into the coffers of Texas elected officials: Scudder, Charlie. "How Lawmakers in Thrall to the NRA Stifle Gun Safety Laws." *The Guardian*, May 27, 2022. https://www.theguardian.com/us-news/2022/may/27/texas -shooting-nra-stifles-gun-regulations.

13. "I have no greater joy than to hear that my children are walking in the truth": 3 John 1:4 (New International Version).

13. "See that you do not despise one of these little ones. For I tell you that their angels in heaven always see the face of my Father in heaven": Matt. 18:10 (New International Version).

13. "If anyone causes one of these little ones—those who believe in me—to stumble, it would be better for them to have a large millstone hung around their neck and to be drowned in the depths of the sea": Matt.18:6 (New International Version).

14. The king was outraged by their disobedience: Dan. 3-6 (New International Version).

15. "The fire had not harmed their bodies, nor was a hair of their heads singed; their robes were not scorched, and there was no smell of fire on them": Dan. 3:27 (New International Version).

17. the twenty-three states that imposed new restrictions on voting in the wake of this decision: Carnegie Corporation of New York. "11 Barriers to Voting." Carnegie Corporation of New York. Accessed November 1, 2019. https://www.carncgie.org/our-work/article/11-barriers-voting/.

18. the proposed district went straight through the Black Belt, and the amicus brief from Alabama historians noted several distinguishing factors: Brief for Alabama Historians as Amici Curiae Supporting Appellee-Respondents, Allen v. Milligan, 599 U.S. 1 (2023) (Nos. 21-1086, 21-1087).

18. Governor Kay Ivey was pleased that the state defied the courts: Daily Kos Elections. "Morning Digest: Alabama Governor Suggests New Map Was Intended to Defy Court Order." *Daily Kos*, July 24, 2023. https://www .dailykos.com/stories/2023/7/24/2182938/-Morning-Digest-Alabama -governor-suggests-new-map-was-intended-to-defy-court-order.

19. State judges would describe the attempts to enact illegal voter-ID laws and undermine access to health care as having been executed with "surgical precision": Ax, Joseph. "North Carolina Court Strikes down State Legislative Map as Unconstitutional Gerrymander." *Reuters*, September 3, 2019. https://www.reuters .com/article/us-north-carolina-gerrymandering/north-carolina -court-strikes-down-state-legislative-map-as-unconstitutional -gerrymander-idUSKCN1VO2MD/.

19. In court, Reverend Barber was questioned by the prosecuting attorney about his behavior at the North Carolina General Assembly: *Democracy Now!* "Rev. William Barber: Racist Gerrymandering Created a GOP Stronghold in the South. We Must Fight Back." *Democracy Now!*, June 11, 2019. https://www.democracynow.org/2019/6/10/rev _william_barber_racist_gerrymandering_created.

21. more than two dozen civil rights leaders in the South had been paid by regional power companies . . . and then became their advocates: Ariza, Mario Alejandro, Kristi E Swartz, and Adam Mahoney. "Power Companies Paid Civil Rights Leaders in the US South. They Became Loyal Industry Advocates." *The Guardian*, January 9, 2024. https://www.theguardian .com/environment/2024/jan/09/power-companies-paid-civil-rights-leaders -in-the-south-they-became-loyal-industry-advocates.

22. a letter to the president and CEO of Duke Energy, calling out this "cynical and duplicitous corporate behavior": Johnson, Nelson, and Jim Warren. Letter to Lynn J. Good. "A Meeting to Discuss Your 'Solar Hurts the Poor' and Anti-Energy Freedom Act Lobbying." *NC WARN*, April 7, 2015. https://www.ncwarn.org/wp-content/uploads/Ltr-4-7-15-to-CEO-Good1 .pdf.

24. "Go Down, Moses" . . . first appeared in sheet music back in 1853, written by a Rev. L. C. Lockwood: Hawn, C. Michael. "History of Hymns: 'Go Down, Moses.'" Discipleship Ministries, The United Methodist Church, March 12, 2019. https://www.umcdiscipleship.org/resources/history-of-hymns-go-down-moses.

24. This is what the Lord, the God of the Hebrews, says: "Let my people go, so that they may worship me": Exod. 9:1 (New International Version).

25. "The Lord, the God of the Hebrews sent me to you to say, 'Let my people go, so that they may worship me in the wilderness'": Exod. 7:16 (New International Version).

2. THE GREAT RURAL DIVIDE

28. for the rural poor in Alabama or Mississippi or South Carolina or Tennessee or Louisiana, which have no state minimum wage requirements, the federal minimum wage of $7.25 an hour still holds: "Brief: State Minimum Wages." National Conference of State Legislatures, April 12, 2024. https://www.ncsl.org/labor-and-employment/state-minimum-wages.

29. Approximately forty-six million Americans live in rural communities in every state of the union: Davis, J. C., Cromartie, J., Farrigan, T., Genetin, B., Sanders, A., & Winikoff, J. B. (2023). *Rural America at a glance: 2023 edition* (Report No. EIB-261). U.S. Department of Agriculture, Economic Research Service. https://doi.org/10.32747/2023.8134362.ers.

30. In urban areas, about 12 percent of residents live below the poverty line; in rural communities that number increases to 15.5 percent: "Nonmetro Poverty Rates Remain Higher Than Metro." USDA Economic Research Service, US Department of Agriculture, February 26, 2024. https://www.ers.usda.gov/data-products/chart-gallery/gallery/chart-detail/?chartId=58300.

30. In those Southern states, the rural poverty rate is close to 20 percent, compared to the 13 percent rate of rural poverty for those who live in the Midwest: "Overview: Rural Poverty & Well-Being." USDA Economic Research Service, US Department of Agriculture, November 15, 2023. https://www.ers.usda.gov/topics/rural-economy-population/rural-poverty-well-being/.

31. poverty has been declining since it was first measured in 1960: Ibid.

31. In my home state of Alabama, out of a total population of just over five million, nearly 1.15 million individuals live in rural communities—and of those rural residents, almost 20 percent are poor: "State Fact Sheets: Alabama." USDA Economic Research Service, US Department of Agriculture, February 7, 2024. https://data.ers.usda.gov/reports.aspx? StateFIPS=01&StateName=Alabama&ID=17854.

31. Lyndon Johnson delivered his first State of the Union address as president: Boteach, Melissa, Erik Stegman, Sarah Baron, Tracey Ross, and Katie Wright. "The War on Poverty: Then and Now." Center for American Progress, January 7, 2014. https://www.americanprogress.org/article /the-war-on-poverty-then-and-now/.

32. Poverty in central Appalachia in 1960 was at 59 percent: Moore, Molly. "Appalachia's Place in the War on Poverty." *The Appalachian Voice*, Appalachian Voices, April 9, 2014. https://appvoices.org/2014/04/09 /appalachias-place-in-the-war-on-poverty/.

32. I read an article about the fiftieth anniversary of his visit: Bello, Marisol. "No Victory in War on Poverty in Eastern Kentucky." *USA Today*, January 25, 2014. https://www.usatoday.com/story/news/nation/2014/01/25 /war-on-poverty-50th-anniversary/4326109/.

32. "Whatever you did for one of the least of these brothers and sisters of mine, you did for me": Matt. 25:40 (New International Version).

33. Jackson, Mississippi, where 28.9 percent of the residents have annual household incomes of less than $25,000: U.S. Census Bureau, "Income in the Past 12 Months (in 2022 Inflation-Adjusted Dollars)," 2022. *American Community Survey, ACS 1-Year Estimates Subject Tables, Table S1901*, 2022, accessed on May 29, 2024, https://data.census.gov/table/ACSST1Y2022 .S1901?g=160XX00US2836000.

34. the *Washington Post* columnist William Raspberry, who wrote a column about Lowndes County: Raspberry, William. "Civil Rights Failure." *Washington Post*, March 17, 2002. https://www.washingtonpost .com/archive/opinions/2002/03/18/civil-rights-failure/e203fe82 -a0f0-4285-9215-617ef3035ae3/.

38. Nearly ten thousand people live there, and, according to the most recent census, 73 percent are Black and about 25 percent are white; 83 percent graduated from high school, while only 17 percent have college degrees: "QuickFacts: Lowndes County, Alabama." U.S. Census Bureau.

Accessed May 29, 2024. https://www.census.gov/quickfacts/fact/table /lowndescountyalabama/PST045222.

39. He was accused of terrible racism, and pilloried for his record on civil rights: Jacobs, Ben. "Jeff Sessions Confirmed as Attorney General Despite Controversies." *The Guardian*, February 9, 2017. https://www.theguardian .com/us-news/2017/feb/08/jeff-sessions-confirmed-attorney-general-senate.

40. Sessions allegedly had said that he had thought there was nothing wrong with Klan members, Figures said, "until he learned that they smoked marijuana": Zamost, Scott, Curt Devine and Katherine Noel. "Sessions Dogged by Old Allegations of Racism." CNN, November 18, 2016. https://www.cnn .com/2016/11/17/politics/jeff-sessions-racism-allegations/index.html.

40. Sessions reportedly had referred to the NAACP, the Southern Christian Leadership Conference, Operation PUSH, and the National Council of Churches as "un-American organizations teaching anti-American values": Ye Hee Lee, Michelle. "Jeff Sessions's Comments on Race: For the Record." *Washington Post*, December 2, 2016. https://www .washingtonpost.com/news/fact-checker/wp/2016/12/02/jeff-sessionss -comments-on-race-for-the-record/.

42. I was invited to testify at a Senate subcommittee hearing on "Rural Water: Modernizing Our Community Water Systems": U.S. Congress. Senate Agriculture, Nutrition, and Forestry Subcommittee on Rural Development and Energy. *Hearings to Examine Rural Water, Focusing on Modernizing Our Community Water Systems*. 118th Cong., July 19, 2023. https://www.agriculture.senate.gov/hearings /rural-water-modernizing-our-community-water-systems.

46. Historian David M. Kennedy in his book *Freedom from Fear: The American People in Depression and War, 1929–1945* quoted the observations of Lorena Hickok: Kennedy, David M. *Freedom From Fear: The American People in Depression and War, 1929–1945*. New York: Oxford University Press, 2005.

48. in Alabama, sharecroppers both white and Black worked three-quarters of the land: Greenberg, Cheryl Lynn. *To Ask for an Equal Chance: African Americans in the Great Depression*. Lanham, MD: Rowman & Littlefield Publishers, Inc, 2011.

49. a circumstance known as "debt peonage": "Slavery v. Peonage." Public Broadcasting Service (PBS). Accessed June 3, 2024. https://www.pbs.org /tpt/slavery-by-another-name/themes/peonage/#.

49. historians have noted that the effects of the Depression in Alabama started earlier and lasted longer than in other parts of the country: "Great Depression in Alabama." Encyclopedia of Alabama, May 11, 2023. https:// encyclopediaofalabama.org/article/great-depression-in-alabama/.

50. By 1927, there were seventy-seven Historically Black Colleges and Universities (HBCUs) educating almost 14,000 students: Redd, Kenneth E. "Historically Black Colleges and Universities: Making a Comeback." *New Directions for Higher Education* 1998, no. 102 (June 1998): 33–43. https://doi .org/10.1002/he.10203.

50. over that period of time, about 219,000 Black farmers who had been share-croppers came to own their land: United States Bureau of the Census. 1933. *Fifteenth Census of the United States: 1930. Census of Agriculture. The Negro Farmer in the United States*. Washington: US GPO.

51. a community known as Prairie Farms was created out of two former plantations: "Prairie Farms Resettlement Community." Encyclopedia of Alabama, May 27, 2023. https://encyclopediaofalabama.org/article /prairie-farms-resettlement-community/.

53. "The truth is that in America today, we have many, many millions of people who are spending 40 to 50 to 60 percent of their limited incomes on housing": Edwards, Brian. "Democratic Presidential Candidate Bernie Sanders Tours the River Region, Decries Inequality across the Area." *Montgomery Advertiser,* May 20, 2019. https://www.montgomeryadvertiser. com/story/news/2019/05/20/democratic-presidential-candidate-bernie -sanders-tours-river-region-decries-inequality-across-area/3745462002/.

53. In a campaign video entitled "Trapped," he reflected on his visit: Bernie Sanders. "Trapped." YouTube, June 18, 2019. https://www.youtube.com /watch?v=EUyfLiNCi3Q.

3. FOOD FOR THE SOUL

63. a remarkable interview with the Queen of Soul, Aretha Franklin: London, Larry, and Aretha Franklin. "Border Crossings: Aretha Franklin." Video. Voice of America (VOA), August 17, 2018. https://www.voanews .com/a/4532874.html.

68. he explains that African American food has been called by a number of dif-ferent names over the centuries: Miller, Adrian. *Soul Food: The Surprising*

Story of an American Cuisine, One Plate at a Time. Chapel Hill: University of North Carolina Press, 2013.

71. President Ronald Reagan declared that ketchup could be considered a vegetable: Bentley, Amy. "Ketchup as a Vegetable." *Gastronomica* 21, no. 1 (2021): 17–26. https://doi.org/10.1525/gfc.2021.21.1.17.

71. In 2023, South Dakota governor Kristi Noem rejected a federal program that would have alleviated food insecurity in the state by providing $7.5 million for poor children, many of them from Indigenous families, to have lunches over the summer: Pfankuch, Bart. "South Dakota Rejects Federal Food Funding Despite 25,000 Children Going Hungry." *South Dakota News Watch*. August 20, 2023. https://www.sdnewswatch.org/south-dakota-rejects-federal-food-funding-kristi-noem/.

72. in the US over the last thirty years, childhood obesity rates have tripled: Obesity Prevention Source. "Child Obesity." Harvard T.H. Chan School of Public Health, April 8, 2016. https://www.hsph.harvard.edu/obesity-prevention-source/obesity-trends-original/global-obesity-trends-in-children/.

72. A report from the Robert Wood Johnson Foundation: Robert Wood Johnson Foundation. "Explore Data by Demographic: Ages 10–17." State of Childhood Obesity, April 18, 2024. https://stateofchildhoodobesity.org/demographic-data/ages-10-17/.

74. A recent study warned that more than 90 percent of fish, shellfish, plants, and algae, not to mention hundreds of species farmed in fresh water, are at risk: Cao, Ling, Benjamin S. Halpern, Max Troell, Rebecca Short, Cong Zeng, Ziyu Jiang, Yue Liu, et al. "Vulnerability of Blue Foods to Human-Induced Environmental Change." *Nature Sustainability* 6, no. 10 (June 26, 2023): 1186–98. https://doi.org/10.1038/s41893-023-01156-y.

75. In 1911, a cookbook appeared entitled *Good Things to Eat, As Suggested by Rufus*: Estes, Rufus, and D. J. Frienz. *Good Things to Eat, as Suggested by Rufus: A collection of Practical Recipes for Preparing Meats, Game, Fowl, Fish, Puddings, Pastries, etc.* Whitefish, MT: Literary Licensing, 2020.

76. It turns out there is a rich and uncertain history about its origins: Galarza, G. Daniela. "Red Velvet Cake Is 'the Color of Joy.' Here's How It Rose into America's Dessert Canon." *Washington Post*, June 11, 2021. https://www.washingtonpost.com/food/2021/06/11/red-velvet-cake-history/.

78. the well-known British chef Jamie Oliver . . . decided to use his fame to help change school meals in the United Kingdom: Jamie Oliver, Fresh One Productions. *Jamie's School Dinners*. Channel 4, United Kingdom, 2005.

78. In 2010, he visited Huntington, West Virginia: Jamie Oliver, Fresh One Productions, Ryan Seacrest, Ryan Seacrest Productions. *Jamie Oliver's Food Revolution*. Season 1. American Broadcasting Company (ABC), 2010.

79. In 2020, researchers from the University of Washington School of Public Health found that since those changes were implemented, the overall nutritional quality of school meals markedly improved: Kinderknecht, Kelsey, Cristen Harris, and Jessica Jones-Smith. "Association of the Healthy, Hunger-Free Kids Act with Dietary Quality among Children in the US National School Lunch Program." *JAMA* 324, no. 4 (July 28, 2020): 359. https://doi.org/10.1001/jama.2020.9517.

80. This network delivered 138,000 pounds of fresh, organic produce to food-insecure families throughout California's Central Coast in a matter of months, and over the year, they provided nearly 850,000 pounds of fresh food throughout the state: Saunders, Lucy. "Growing the Table Provides Free, Organic Produce to Farmworkers' Families and People Experiencing Homelessness." Growing the Table, September 24, 2021. https://www .growingthetable.org/news/growing-the-table-provides-free-organic -produce-to-farmworkers-families-and-people-experiencing-homelessness.

4. THE MEANING OF LIFE

84. as "Mississippi appendectomies": Kugler, Sara. "Mississippi Appendectomies and Reproductive Justice." MSNBC, March 27, 2014. https://www.msnbc .com/msnbc/day-17-mississippi-appendectomies-msna293361.

84. In Hamer's case, she had gone to the hospital to have a uterine tumor removed in 1961: Michals, Debra, ed. "Fannie Lou Hamer." National Women's History Museum, 2017. https://www.womenshistory.org /education-resources/biographies/fannie-lou-hamer.

84. As a Mississippi congressman had reportedly said, forced sterilization was designed to "stop this black tide which threatens to engulf us": The Council of Federated Organizations, *The Mississippi Legislature—1964*. Jackson, MS: The Council of Federated Organization, 1964, p. 31. https://www.crmvet .org/docs/6406_cofo_ms_leg-rpt.pdf.

85. 100,000 to 150,000 poor and mostly Black and Native women were sterilized *every year* until 1979: Southern Poverty Law Center. "Relf v. Weinberger." Southern Poverty Law Center. Accessed May 29, 2024. https://www.splcenter .org/seeking-justice/case-docket/relf-v-weinberger.

85. immoral experiments conducted by the US Public Health Service and the Communicable Disease Center on almost four hundred Black men who suffered from syphilis were entering their thirty-third year: Urell, Aaryn. "Tuskegee Syphilis Experiment." Equal Justice Initiative, October 31, 2020. https://eji.org/news/history-racial-injustice -tuskegee-syphilis-experiment/.

86. In some teaching hospitals, poor Black women were not told what was taking place: Roberts, Dorothy E. *Killing the Black Body: Race, Reproduction, and the Meaning of Liberty*. New York: Vintage, 1999.

86. on July 17, 1973, when the Southern Poverty Law Center filed a lawsuit on behalf of two mentally disabled sisters, Mary Alice and Minnie Lee Relf: Southern Poverty Law Center. "Relf v. Weinberger." Southern Poverty Law Center. Accessed May 29, 2024. https://www.splcenter.org /seeking-justice/case-docket/relf-v-weinberger.

91. Judge Gerhard Gesell . . . wrote in his decision, "The dividing line between family planning and eugenics is murky": Schmeck, Harold M. "Court Curbs U.S. on Sterilization." *New York Times*, March 16, 1974. https://www .nytimes.com/1974/03/16/archives/court-curbs-us-on-sterilization-special -to-the-new-york-times.html.

91. Two hundred twenty women in North Carolina received about $45,000: Associated Press. "Final Compensation Check Sent to NC Sterilization Victims." *AP News*, February 8, 2018. https://apnews.com /b40b5584543d498fb1fea29b97aced4e.

91. In Virginia, the victims were given $25,000: Garcia, Catherine. "Victims of Forced Sterilization Receive $25,000 Each from the State of Virginia." *The Week*, February 27, 2015. https://theweek.com/speedreads/541477 /victims-forced-sterilization-receive-25000-each-from-state-virginia.

91. In 2022, the state legislature created the California Forced or Involuntary Sterilized Compensation Program: "California Launches Program to Compensate Survivors of State-Sponsored Sterilization." Office of Governor Gavin Newsom, December 31, 2021. Governor of California. https://www.gov.ca.gov/2021/12/31/california-launches-program-to -compensate-survivors-of-state-sponsored-sterilization/.

92. Minnie Lee and Mary Alice, now in their sixties, survive on their Social Security checks: Villarosa, Linda. "The Long Shadow of Eugenics in America." *New York Times*, June 8, 2022. https://www.nytimes.com /2022/06/08/magazine/eugenics-movement-america.html.

94. antiabortion legislatures all over the country have engaged in an orgy of restrictions on basic health care for women: Felix, Mabel, Laurie Sobel, and Alina Salganicoff. "A Review of Exceptions in State Abortion Bans: Implications for the Provision of Abortion Services." KFF Women's Health Policy, May 18, 2023. https://www.kff.org/womens-health -policy/issue-brief/a-review-of-exceptions-in-state-abortions-bans -implications-for-the-provision-of-abortion-services/.

94. Representative John Becker from Ohio . . . authored legislation in which surgery for abortion services would be covered by health insurance only to save a woman's life: Garrand, Danielle. "This Ohio Anti-Abortion Bill Says That Ectopic Pregnancies Can Be Moved to the Uterus—But That Isn't Scientifically Possible." *CBS News*, May 16, 2019. https://www .cbsnews.com/news/ohio-abortion-ectopic-pregnancy-bill-this-ohio-anti -abortion-bill-says-that-ectopic-pregnancies-can-be-moved/.

95. On February 16, 2024, the court ruled, in an 8–1 decision, that the embryos were minors: LePage v. Center for Reproductive Medicine, P.C., SC-2022- 0515; SC-2022-0579 (Ala. 2024).

96. our Republican-dominated state legislature immediately passed a law that offered "civil and criminal immunity for death or dam- age to an embryo to any individual or entity when providing or re- ceiving goods or services related to in vitro fertilization": Edelman, Adam. "Alabama Governor Signs Bill to Protect IVF Treatments into Law." NBCNews, March 6, 2024. https://www.nbcnews.com/politics /alabama-lawmakers-ivf-protection-bill-vote-rcna141710.

96. a single IVF cycle running about $23,000; many patients require more than one cycle . . . the average patient will spend close to $50,000 in treatment: FertilityIQ, "The Cost of IVF by City." Inflection, accessed May 29, 2024. https://www.fertilityiq.com/fertilityiq/articles/the-cost-of-ivf-by-city.

96. a nurse named Dawn Wooten, who worked at the Irwin County Detention Center in Ocilla, Georgia, filed a whistle-blower complaint: Government Accountability Project. "Nurse Dawn Wooten." Government Accountability Project, October 4, 2023. https://whistleblower.org /whistleblower-profiles/nurse-dawn-wooten/.

96. Dr. Amin spoke no Spanish, and many of the vulnerable, detained women he violated spoke no English: Dickerson, Caitlin, Seth Freed Wessler, and Miriam Jordan. "Immigrants Say They Were Pressured into Unneeded Surgeries." *New York Times*, September 29, 2020. https://www.nytimes .com/2020/09/29/us/ice-hysterectomies-surgeries-georgia.html.

97. A congressional investigation finally revealed that "female detainees appear to have undergone excessive, invasive, and often unnecessary gynecological procedures": Montoya-Galvez, Camilo. "Investigation Finds Women Detained by ICE Underwent 'Unnecessary Gynecological Procedures' at Georgia Facility." *CBS News*, November 15, 2022. https://www.cbsnews .com/news/women-detained-ice-unnecessary-gynecological-procedures -georgia-facility-investigation/.

5. MIGRATIONS, FORCED AND FREE

102. Dr. Craig Venter . . . announced the findings of the Human Genome Project at the White House in 2000: Kolbert, Elizabeth. "There's No Scientific Basis for Race—It's a Made-up Label." *National Geographic,* The Race Issue, April 2018.

103. David Reich, a Harvard paleogeneticist, told *National Geographic* that in some populations, genetic differences have been rendered nearly irrelevant because of migration: Ibid.

107. a terrible, coordinated terrorist attack had taken place in the city, killing 130 people and wounding 600 others: Rubin, Alissa J., and Elian Peltier. "The Paris Attacks, 2 Years Later: Quiet Remembrance and Lasting Impact." *New York Times*, November 13, 2017. https://www.nytimes.com/2017/11/13 /world/europe/paris-november-2015.html.

107. a report from the Department of Environment and Climate Change in Nova Scotia: Rep. *Weathering What's Ahead: Climate Change Risk and Nova Scotia's Well-Being.* Department of Environment and Climate Change, Province of Nova Scotia, December 2022. https://climatechange.novascotia .ca/sites/default/files/uploads/climate-change-risk-report.pdf.

108. The British medical journal *The Lancet* warned that of all the capitals in Europe facing extreme heat, Paris was the most vulnerable and its population faced the highest risk of heat-related deaths: Masselot, Pierre, Malcolm Mistry, Jacopo Vanoli, Rochelle Schneider, Tamara Iungman, David Garcia-Leon, Juan-Carlos Ciscar, et al. "Excess Mortality Attributed

to Heat and Cold: A Health Impact Assessment Study in 854 Cities in Europe." *The Lancet Planetary Health* 7, no. 4 (April 2023). https://doi .org/10.1016/s2542-5196(23)00023-2.

108. In 2022, months of catastrophic rainfall from the summer through the early fall impacted Nigeria, Chad, Niger, and surrounding countries . . . killing more than 1,500 and displacing approximately 3.2 million more: Rep. *West and Central Africa: Flooding Situation—as of 15 December 2022.* UN Office for the Coordination of Humanitarian Affairs (OCHA), December 2022. https://reliefweb.int/report/nigeria /west-and-central-africa-flooding-situation-15-december-2022.

110. As *The Guardian* reported, "Children playing feet away from open pools of raw sewage": Pilkington, Ed. "Hookworm, a Disease of Extreme Poverty, Is Thriving in the US South. Why?" *The Guardian.* September 5, 2017. https://www.theguardian.com/us-news/2017/sep /05/hookworm-lowndes-county-alabama-water-waste-treatment-poverty.

110. Heat-related deaths in West Africa are projected to be up to nine times higher than in the period from 1950 to 2005: Rep. *The IPCC's Sixth Assessment Report: Impacts, Adaptation Options and Investment Areas for a Climate-Resilient West Africa.* Climate and Development Knowledge Network (CDKN) Programme and African Climate & Development Initiative (ACDI), 2022. https://cdkn.org/sites/default/files/2022-03 /IPCC%20Regional%20Factsheet%202_West%20Africa_web.pdf.

111. Oxfam reported that "the richest one percent of the world population produced as much carbon pollution in 2019 than the five billion people who made up the poorest two-thirds of humanity": "Richest 1% Emit as Much Planet-Heating Pollution as Two-Thirds of Humanity." Oxfam International, November 20, 2023. https://www.oxfam.org/en/press-releases /richest-1-emit-much-planet-heating-pollution-two-thirds-humanity#.

112. "After the final no, there comes a yes, and on that yes the future world depends": Stevens, Wallace, Joan Richardson, and Frank Kermode, eds. "The Well Dressed Man with a Beard." Poem. In *Wallace Stevens: Collected Poetry and Prose.* New York: Library of America, 1997.

6. MY MOON SHOT

116. Dr. King had been planning another Poor People's Campaign march, as an effort to find the "middle ground between riots on the one hand and

timid supplications for justice on the other": "Poor People's Campaign." The Martin Luther King, Jr. Research and Education Institute, Stanford University. Accessed May 29, 2024. https://kinginstitute.stanford.edu /poor-peoples-campaign.

116. Their success was modest: funds for free and reduced lunches were allocated after the demonstrations and much-needed Head Start programs were established in Mississippi and Alabama: "1968: The Year That Changed America." Google Arts & Culture. Accessed May 29, 2024. https:// artsandculture.google.com/story/1968-the-year-that-changed-america /ggUBmE4X0VXGIA?hl=en.

117. On the evening of July 14, 1969— less than a week before the first moon landing—about five hundred marchers arrived at NASA's gates in Florida: Niiler, Eric. "Why Civil Rights Activists Protested the Moon Landing." History.com, July 11, 2019. https://www.history.com/news /apollo-11-moon-landing-launch-protests.

118. In response, Paine said, "If we could solve the problems of poverty in the United States by not pushing the button to launch men to the moon tomorrow, then we would not push that button": Heppenheimer, T. A. *The Space Shuttle Decision: NASA's Search for a Reusable Space Vehicle*. Washington, DC: NASA, 1999. https://www.nasa.gov/wp-content/uploads/2023/04 /sp-4221.pdf.

119. In 1958, President Dwight D. Eisenhower created NASA by signing the National Aeronautics and Space Act: "60 Years and Counting: President Eisenhower Signs NASA into Existence." NASA. Accessed May 29, 2024. https://www.nasa.gov/specials/signing/.

120. In what became known as Operation Paperclip, these engineers, physicists, and highly skilled technicians were able to shed their Nazi past and receive secret government jobs in the United States: Neufeld, Michael. "Project Paperclip and American Rocketry after World War II." National Air and Space Museum, March 31, 2023. https://airandspace.si.edu/stories/editorial /project-paperclip-and-american-rocketry-after-world-war-ii#.

120. A group of more than a hundred of them were moved to Redstone Arsenal in Huntsville in 1950: Dewan, Shaila. "When the Germans, and Rockets, Came to Town." *New York Times*, December 31, 2007. https://www.nytimes .com/2007/12/31/us/31huntsville.html.

120. The leader of this group, the most valuable asset of all, was a former member of the Nazi party and the SS, an aerospace engineer named Wernher

von Braun: "Wernher von Braun." NASA. Accessed May 29, 2024. https://
www.nasa.gov/people/wernher-von-braun/.

121. More than sixty thousand prisoners—of course, mostly Jews—were
forced to work here, with more than a third dying from the punishing demands, torture at the hands of the guards, starvation, or disease:
Neufeld, Michael. "'Wonder Weapons' and Slave Labor." National Air and
Space Museum, June 23, 2020. https://airandspace.si.edu/stories/editorial
/wonder-weapons-and-slave-labor.

122. Only 16,437 people lived in the city at the time . . . the approximately five thousand Black people who lived there: Robinson, Kerry. "Blacks in Huntsville,
Alabama, Sit in and Win Racial Desegregation at Lunch Counters, 1962."
Global Nonviolent Action Database, Swarthmore College, April 14,
2014. https://nvdatabase.swarthmore.edu/content/blacks-huntsville
-alabama-sit-and-win-racial-desegregation-lunch-counters-1962.

122. the population more than quadrupled to seventy-two thousand in
just ten years: "1960 Census of Population: Volume 1. Characteristics
of the Population: Part 2. Alabama, Chapter B. General Population
Characteristics." U.S. Census Bureau, October 8, 2021. https://www2
.census.gov/library/publications/decennial/1960/population-volume-1
/vol-01-02-d.pdf.

123. In 1962, a group of these leaders created the Community Service Committee:
PBS, American Experience. "The Desegregation of Huntsville." YouTube,
June 27, 2019. https://www.youtube.com/watch?v=KR0f5Kf6-mo.

123. In March 1962, the local leaders invited Dr. King to Huntsville to speak
at what was then Oakwood College . . . and the First Missionary Baptist
Church: Seale, Michael. "MLK's Iconic 'I Have a Dream' Speech Has
Origins in Huntsville." Hville Blast, January 16, 2023. https://hvilleblast
.com/mlks-iconic-i-have-a-dream-speech-in-huntsville/.

123. two new, sympathetic figures appeared at the local lunch counter: Martha
Hereford, a very pregnant doctor's wife, and Joan Cashin, a dentist's
wife who was holding her four-month-old baby: Robinson, Kerry.
"Blacks in Huntsville, Alabama, Sit in and Win Racial Desegregation
at Lunch Counters, 1962." Global Nonviolent Action Database,
Swarthmore College, April 14, 2014. https://nvdatabase.swarthmore.edu
/content/blacks-huntsville-alabama-sit-and-win-racial-desegregation
-lunch-counters-1962.

124. Sonnie Hereford IV's momentous appearance in the first grade of Fifth Avenue Elementary School: "'Why Not My Son?' How Sonnie Hereford IV and His Dad Integrated Alabama's Public Schools." Southern Poverty Law Center, September 7, 2018. https://www.splcenter.org /news/2018/09/07/why-not-my-son-how-sonnie-hereford-iv-and-his -dad-integrated-alabamas-public-schools.

124. the Huntsville dentist . . . was also one of the founders of the National Democratic Party of Alabama, which facilitated the election of more than a hundred Black people to public office in Alabama from 1968 to 1974: "Dr. John Cashin's Biography." The HistoryMakers, April 24, 2007. https:// www.thehistorymakers.org/biography/dr-john-cashin-41.

125. the PBS series about the space race, *Chasing the Moon*: Moss, Steven, and Richard Paul. "Wernher von Braun's Record on Civil Rights." PBS American Experience, May 11, 2019. https://www.pbs.org/wgbh /americanexperience/features/chasing-moon-von-braun-record -on-civil-rights/.

125. In 1965 Alabama's white supremacist governor, George C. Wallace, decided to appear at the NASA headquarters in Huntsville with reporters: Ibid.

126. in 1982 after having survived an assassination attempt that left him paralyzed from the waist down, Wallace met with civil rights leaders and apologized: Bragg, Rick. "Emotional March Gains a Repentant Wallace." *New York Times*, March 11, 1995. https://www.nytimes.com/1995/03/11/us /emotional-march-gains-a-repentant-wallace.html.

126. In 1987 he even reconciled with Rev. Jesse Jackson: "Jackson Courts Wallace for Support in South." *Chicago Tribune*, July 21, 1987. https://www .chicagotribune.com/1987/07/21/jackson-courts-wallace-for-support-in -south/.

127. When the Marshall Space Flight Center was established in 1960, Huntsville was fifty-one square miles and home to 72,365 people, 14 percent of whom were Black residents: Ibid., 10.

127. By 2023, Huntsville was the largest city in Alabama, with 235,204 residents—30 percent of whom are Black: "QuickFacts: Huntsville City, Alabama." U.S. Census Bureau. Accessed May 29, 2024. https:// www.census.gov/quickfacts/fact/table/huntsvillecityalabama,US /BZA115221.

127. but if you include the entire metropolitan area, now a sprawling 1,300 square miles, that population soars to 500,000: "QuickFacts: Madison

County, Alabama; Limestone County, Alabama." U.S. Census Bureau. Accessed May 29, 2024. https://www.census.gov/quickfacts/fact/table /madisoncountyalabama,limestonecountyalabama,US/BZA115221.

127. Marilyn Lands won 62.31 percent of the vote to replace a Republican who had to resign after pleading guilty to voter fraud: Richards, Zoë. "Democrat Marilyn Lands Wins Alabama Special Election after IVF, Abortion Rights Campaigning." NBC News, March 26, 2024. https://www.nbcnews. com/politics/elections/democrat-marilyn-lands-wins-alabama-special -election-ivf-abortion-righ-rcna145210.

127. a *60 Minutes* story about me and my environmental justice work: Whitaker, Bill. "60 Minutes Investigates: Americans Fighting for Access to Sewage Disposal." CBS News, December 19, 2021. https://www.cbsnews.com/news /alabama-sewage-disposal-60-minutes-2021-12-19/.

128. Since 1979, NASA has charted the rise in carbon dioxide and methane and the concomitant rise in global temperature and the precipitous decline of Arctic Sea ice: "Arctic Sea Ice Minimum Extent." NASA, October 23, 2023. https://climate.nasa.gov/vital-signs/arctic-sea-ice/?intent=121.

128. The storied British boarding school Eton . . . had to close down in January 2024 because flooding in the river Thames so stressed the sewage system that the toilets couldn't function: Mather, Victor. "Blocked Toilets Close Eton, Boarding School for Britain's Elite Sons." *New York Times*, January 10, 2024. https://www.nytimes.com/2024/01/10/world/europe/eton-college -flooding-toilets.html.

129. the climate crisis will lead to an additional 14.5 million deaths: "Climate Crisis May Cause 14.5 Million Deaths by 2050." World Economic Forum, January 16, 2024. https://www.weforum.org/press/2024/01 /wef24-climate-crisis-health/.

7. HOLY GROUND

131. the thousands of Black people who were, in his words, "drowned, burned, shot, and hanged" in the Jim Crow South: Equal Justice Initiative. "Dedication of the National Memorial for Peace and Justice." YouTube, October 29, 2018. https://www.youtube.com/watch?v=1pUNPAsI6zc.

132. They were able to document 4,400 individuals who lost their lives to racial violence: "Lynching in America: Confronting the Legacy of Racial Terror

(3d Ed., 2017)." Equal Justice Initiative. Accessed May 31, 2024. https://lynchinginamerica.eji.org/report/.

132. Mary Turner, was pregnant when she spoke out against the white mob who had lynched her husband: "May 19, 1918: Mary Turner, Pregnant, Lynched in Georgia for Criticizing Husband's Lynching." Equal Justice Initiative. Accessed May 31, 2024. https://calendar.eji.org/racial-injustice/may/19.

133. "In the soil is the blood of those who were lynched": Ibid., 1.

135. A large blue plaque emblazoned with gold letters states, "LYNCHING IN LETO-HATCHEE": "Lynching in America / Lynching in Letohatchee: Community Remembrance Project." The Historical Marker Database, September 20, 2016. https://www.hmdb.org/m.asp?m=97983.

135. the stories of the seven victims in Letohatchee, Alabama, are laid out: "Community Historical Marker Project." Equal Justice Initiative, August 12, 2022. https://eji.org/projects/community-historical-marker-project/.

136. a historic marker on the right, this one with white letters against a black background: "Holy Ground Battlefield." The Historical Marker Database, August 3, 2016. https://www.hmdb.org/m.asp?m=60714.

139. the anthropologist Gregory A. Waselkov recounted the long history of the Creeks interacting with Europeans: Waselkov, Gregory A. *A Conquering Spirit: Fort Mims and the Redstick War of 1813–1814.* Tuscaloosa: University of Alabama Press, 2009.

140. Hundreds of people were killed, and the property was burned: "History of Fort Mims." Alabama Historical Commission (AHC). Accessed May 29, 2024. https://ahc.alabama.gov/FtMimsHistoryFacts.aspx.

141. twenty-three million acres of land that the Creek people once claimed as their own . . . was surrendered to the white settlers: Glass, Andrew. "Andrew Jackson Signs Peace Treaty with Creek Indians, Aug. 9, 1814." *Politico*, August 8, 2015. https://www.politico.com/story/2015/08/jackson-signs-peace-treaty-with-creek-indians-aug-9-1814-121182.

142. President Andrew Jackson forced as many as a hundred thousand Native Americans to give up their homes: National Geographic Society. "The Indian Removal Act and the Trail of Tears." National Geographic Education, January 29, 2024. https://education.nationalgeographic.org/resource/indian-removal-act-and-trail-tears/.

144. this iconic image of a well-dressed, dignified Black woman, battered and bruised: "Amelia Boynton." SNCC Digital Gateway, April 25, 2018. https://snccdigital.org/people/amelia-boynton/.

8. THIS IS WHAT DISINVESTMENT LOOKS LIKE

149. the 1955 murder of Emmett Till, the fourteen-year-old boy from Chicago whose visit to his grandparents in the Mississippi Delta resulted in a historic tragedy: "Emmett Till's Death Inspired a Movement." National Museum of African American History and Culture, February 29, 2024. https://nmaahc .si.edu/explore/stories/emmett-tills-death-inspired-movement.

150. The film tells the story of the 1964 murder of three civil rights workers: Parker, Alan. *Mississippi Burning*. Orion Pictures, 1988. 128 minutes.

151. the ancestral home of the Choctaw, who in the 1830s were among the first native people forcibly relocated by President Andrew Jackson's Indian removal program: "The Trail of Tears: Why We Remember." Choctaw Nation of Oklahoma, July 5, 2023. https://www.choctawnation.com /biskinik/news/the-trail-of-tears-why-we-remember/.

152. Only in 1967, after the Department of Justice leveled federal charges, were eighteen people held accountable of civil rights violations: Barrouquere, Brett. "The Last Days of a Klansman: Edgar Ray Killen Remained a Defiant Racist in Prison until the End." Southern Poverty Law Center, March 21, 2018. https://www.splcenter.org/hatewatch/2018/03/21/last-days -klansman-edgar-ray-killen-remained-defiant-racist-prison-until-end.

153. On January 4, 1965, when the Eighty-Ninth US Congress was called into session, these brave men and women traveled to Washington to object to the swearing in of the delegation from Mississippi: "MFDP Congressional Challenge." SNCC Digital Gateway, September 24, 2021. https://snccdigital .org/events/mfdp-congressional-challenge/.

154. Stokely Carmichael, by then a leading figure in the movement, described that day: "The 1965 Mississippi Congressional Challenge." Civil Rights Teaching. https://www.civilrightsteaching.org/resource/1965-mississippi -congressional-challenge#.

156. From 2000 to 2010, 19,485 white residents left the city, while 7,976 Black residents settled there—and the population dropped 5.8 percent in that period, from 184,256 in 2000 to 173,514 in 2010: Schaefer, Ward. "Jackson 'White Flight' Slows in Last Decade." *Jackson Free Press*, March 16, 2011. https://www.jacksonfreepress.com/news/2011/mar/16 /jackson-white-flight-slows-in-last-decade/#.

156. By 2023 there were fewer than 150,000 residents . . . white people . . . make up around fifteen percent: "QuickFacts: Jackson, Mississippi." U.S. Census

Bureau. Accessed May 29, 2024. https://www.census.gov/quickfacts/fact
/table/jacksoncitymississippi/PST045223.

157. To some, Lumumba isn't expected to merely disrupt the status quo. He's expected to shatter it": Vicory, Justin. "What Has Chokwe Antar Lumumba
Accomplished in First 100 Days?" *Mississippi Clarion Ledger*, October 18,
2017. https://www.clarionledger.com/story/news/local/2017/10/18
/first-100-days-how-jackson-mayor-lumumba-doing/711858001/.

157. Lumumba managed to secure a $600 million water improvement allo-
cation from the EP: "Mayor Lumumba, Partners Secure Nearly $800
Million in Aid for Jackson's Troubled Water System." The City of Jackson,
Mississippi, January 6, 2023. https://ww2.jacksonms.gov/mayor-lumumba
-partners-secure-nearly-800-million-in-aid-for-jacksons-troubled
-water-system/.

158. The NAACP filed a Title VI civil rights complaint in 2022: "NAACP
Files Discrimination Complaint for Mishandling of Jackson Water
Crisis." NAACP, September 27, 2022. https://naacp.org/articles
/naacp-files-discrimination-complaint-mishandling-jackson
-water-crisis.

158. *Politico* pointed out in a 2021 profile of him as he was preparing for his successful re-election campaign: Rayasam, Renuka.
"How a 'Radical' Southern Mayor Ran up against Reality." *Politico*,
March 31, 2021. https://www.politico.com/news/magazine/2021/03/31
/chokwe-antar-lumumba-jackson-progressives-478380.

159. On October 5, 1963, the front page of the *Clarion-Ledger* announced "Dam
Sluice Gates Are Open for Ross Barnett Reservoir: "Dam Sluice Gates Are
Open for Ross Barnett Reservoir." *The Clarion-Ledger*. October 5, 1963, Vol.
CXXV, No. 237 edition.

160. In 1993, the city's primary water plant, the O.B. Curtis Plant, was built near
the reservoir, and there it remained without sufficient upgrades for twenty
years: McBride, Earnest. "Jackson's Water System: How Did We Get Here?
And How Does It Get Fixed?" Jackson Advocate, January 10, 2022. https://
jacksonadvocateonline.com/jacksons-water-system-how-did-we-get-here
-and-how-does-it-get-fixed-2/.

160. In 2010, several water mains broke during an intense winter storm: Brown,
Robbie. "Frigid Temperatures in South Are Putting Pipes and Patience
to the Test." *New York Times*, January 12, 2010. https://www.nytimes
.com/2010/01/12/us/12jackson.html.

160. Another water main break in 2016 that officials did not, or could not, repair for seven years left a massive ditch filled with water next to a golf course: Fowler, Sarah. "A Water System So Broken That One Pipe Leaks 5 Million Gallons a Day." *New York Times*, March 22, 2023. https://www.nytimes.com/2023/03/22/us/jackson-mississippi-water-crisis.html#:~.

160. From January until March of 2020, Jackson was inundated with a record amount of rainfall. . . . Nearly a half billion—yes, with a *b*—gallons of raw or barely treated sewage ended up in the Pearl River: Vicory, Justin. "Half-billion Gallons of Jackson Sewage Overflowed into Pearl River, Report Shows." *Mississippi Clarion Ledger*, June 1, 2020. https://www.clarionledger.com/story/news/2020/06/01/sewage-pearl-river-jackson-overflow-rain/5282301002/.

161. The bill passed the state legislature only to be vetoed by Gov. Tate Reeves: "Gov. Reeves Vetoes Bill to Help Jackson Collect Delinquent Water Accounts." WJTV, June 30, 2020. https://www.wjtv.com/news/gov-reeves-vetoes-bill-to-help-jackson-collect-delinquent-water-accounts/.

161. since 1980, the average cost of water service increased by 285 percent in Detroit and 320 percent in Flint: Rahman, Nushrat. "Water Is Unaffordable across Michigan, Study Shows." *Detroit Free Press*, December 15, 2021. https://www.freep.com/story/news/local/michigan/2021/12/15/water-unaffordable-michigan-report-study/8890089002/.

161. in 2014, poor and low-income people were unable to keep up with these rising costs and ended up with their water being shut off if their bills were more than sixty days overdue or if they owed more than $150: Kurth, Joel. "Detroit Cites Progress, but Water Shutoffs Actually Rose Last Year." *Bridge Michigan*, May 2, 2017. https://www.bridgemi.com/urban-affairs/detroit-cites-progress-water-shutoffs-actually-rose-last-year.

161. Only after a lawsuit filed by the ACLU and the NAACP in July 2020 did the city of Detroit address the problem with subsidies and caps on charges: "Water Shutoffs in Detroit." ACLU of Michigan, December 19, 2023. https://www.aclumich.org/en/cases/water-shutoffs-detroit.

162. another freak winter storm hit in 2021: Wolf, Zachary B. "Everyone Knew Jackson's Water Crisis Was Coming." CNN, August 30, 2022. https://www.cnn.com/2022/08/30/politics/jackson-mississippi-water-system-what-matters/index.html.

162. In August 2022, unusually heavy rainfall caused the Pearl River to flood, and once more the crumbling infrastructure collapsed: Wagster Pettus,

Emily and Michael Goldberg. "Mississippi Capital: Water Everywhere, Not a Drop to Drink." AP News, August 31, 2022. https://apnews.com /article/floods-mississippi-tate-reeves-jackson-climate-and-environment -3cc65dd4bdc83e8c48a7aeee8b76bd8d.

162. "We don't have water. Water means we don't have air-conditioning. We can't use toilets. We don't have water, therefore we don't have ice, which pretty much places a burden on the program," he said: Davis, Scott. "Deion Sanders Helped Move the Jackson State Football Team out of Town Amid the City's Clean Water Crisis." *Business Insider,* August 31, 2022. https://www .businessinsider.com/jackson-ms-water-crisis-deion-sanders-moves -football-team-off-campus-2022-8#.

163. Only a few months later, during Jackson State University's homecoming game, a time when thousands of people descend on the city, the water system nearly collapsed under the strain: Simmons, Scott. "JSU Homecoming Put Strain on Jackson's Water System, Mayor Says." WAPT, October 25, 2022. https://www.wapt.com/article/jsu-homecoming-put-strain-on-jacksons -water-system-mayor-says/41767610.

163. President Joe Biden declared a ninety-day state of emergency and authorized federal funds to cover the costs: "President Joseph R. Biden, Jr. Approves Mississippi Emergency Declaration." The White House, August 30, 2022. https://www.whitehouse.gov/briefing-room /presidential-actions/2022/08/30/president-joseph-r-biden-jr-approves -mississippi-emergency-declaration-2/.

163. the Department of Justice alleged that Jackson had failed to comply with the Safe Drinking Water Act, and, in a settlement, a federal court order appointed what was referred to as an "interim third-party manager" of the water system: "United States Files Complaint and Reaches Agreement on Proposal with City of Jackson and State of Mississippi on Interim Solution to the Jackson Water Crisis." U.S. Department of Justice Office of Public Affairs, November 29, 2022. U.S. Department of Justice (DOJ). https://www.justice.gov/opa/pr/united-states-files-complaint-and-reaches -agreement-proposal-city-jackson-and-state.

163. in May 2023, the Southern Poverty Law Center filed a complaint to the US Treasury, alleging that the state legislature again made it nearly impossible for the city to access the funds they needed: Southern Poverty Law Center on behalf of residents of Jackson, Mississippi. Gutman, Miriam, Jamie Rush, Malissa Williams, Crystal Stevens McElrath, and

Kirsten Anderson. "Title VI Complaint to Treasury regarding MDEQ." Southern Poverty Law Center, May 2, 2023. https://www.splcenter.org/sites /default/files/title-vi-complaint-to-treasury-regarding-mdeq.pdf.

164. problems with the water supply still persisted, and community members were also frustrated with the lack of transparency, information, or input they had in the process of resolving the water crisis: "In re: Safe Drinking Water Act in Jackson, Mississippi." Center for Constitutional Rights, March 20, 2024. https://ccrjustice.org/home/what-we-do/our-cases /re-safe-drinking-water-act-jackson-mississippi.

9. FOR THE LOVE OF MY PEOPLE

165. 15,400 people lived in Lowndes County, with eighty-six white families owning 90 percent of the land: "Lowndes County Freedom Party." Encyclopedia of Alabama, October 5, 2023. https://encyclopediaofalabama .org/article/lowndes-county-freedom-organization/.

166. civil rights activist Stokely Carmichael and nine others were arrested in Prattville: Freedom Information Service. "Mississippi Newsletter No. 18." Civil Rights Movement Archive, June 23, 1967. https://www.crmvet .org/docs/fis/670623_ms_newsletter.pdf.

167. An SNCC news release reported, "At about 4 a.m. police ordered those in the house outside.": Freedom Information Service. "Mississippi Newsletter No. 18." Civil Rights Movement Archive, June 23, 1967. https://www.crmvet.org/docs/fis/670623_ms_newsletter.pdf

167. the site where the Interpretive Center now sits was transformed from an open field into a massive tent city: "After the March—Tent City Historical Marker: Selma to Montgomery National Historic Trail." The Historical Marker Database, November 9, 2021. https://www.hmdb.org/m.asp?m=112405.

169. During the 1965 Selma to Montgomery march, the Lowndes County Freedom Party was formed to organize Black voters there: "Lowndes County Freedom Party (LCFP)." SNCC Digital Gateway, May 1, 2018. https://snccdigital.org/inside-sncc/alliances-relationships/lcfp/.

169. Get-out-the-vote posters of the time . . . posed the question, "Is this the party you want?": pamphlet by the Lowndes County Freedom Organization. University of North Texas Libraries, UNT Digital Library, UNT Libraries Special Collections, 1964/1966. https://digital.library.unt.edu/ark:/67531 /metadc1884472/.

172. we worked with the organization Earthjustice to file our first complaint using Title VI of the Civil Rights Act: Earthjustice on behalf of Alabama Center for Rural Enterprise. Sewell, Anna, and Neil Gormley. "Re: Complaint Under Title VI of the Civil Rights Act of 1964, 42 U.S.C. § 2000d, 45, C.F.R. Part 80." Earthjustice, September 28, 2018. https://earthjustice.org/wp-content/uploads/acre20title20vi20complaint20with20exhibits_09-28-2018.pdf.

173. a *New York Times* op-ed written by Dr. Peter Hotez, a tropical and infectious disease specialist at Baylor College of Medicine in Houston: Hotez, Peter J. "Tropical Diseases: The New Plague of Poverty." *New York Times*, August 19, 2012, sec. SR. https://www.nytimes.com/2012/08/19/opinion/sunday/tropical-diseases-the-new-plague-of-poverty.html.

174. a meticulous peer-reviewed study that took nearly three years . . . found that 34.5 percent of the adults and children in the community tested positive for parasitic intestinal worms: McKenna, Megan L., Shannon McAtee, Patricia E. Bryan, Rebecca Jeun, Tabitha Ward, Jacob Kraus, Maria E. Bottazzi, Peter J. Hotez, Catherine C. Flowers, and Rojelio Mejia. "Human Intestinal Parasite Burden and Poor Sanitation in Rural Alabama." *The American Journal of Tropical Medicine and Hygiene* 97, no. 5 (November 8, 2017): 1623–28. https://doi.org/10.4269/ajtmh.17-0396.

174. in May 2023, came another historic development: the DOJ and HHS reached an interim settlement with the Alabama Department of Public Health: U.S. Department of Justice. *Interim Resolution Agreement Between the United States Department of Justice And the United States Department of Health and Human Services and the Alabama Department of Public Health.* Department of Justice Number 171-3-14; Department of Health and Human Services Office for Civil Rights Transaction Number 22-451932. U.S. Department of Justice Office of Public Affairs, May 4, 2023. https://www.justice.gov/opa/press-release/file/1582566/dl?inline.

180. The case went all the way to the Supreme Court, who, in a 5–4 decision, permitted the state to execute him: de Vogue, Ariane. "5–4 Supreme Court Clears the Way for Alabama Execution." CNN, January 27, 2022. https://www.cnn.com/2022/01/27/politics/supreme-court-death-penalty-matthew-reeves-alabama/index.html.

184. When Assistant Attorney General Kristen Clarke . . . announced the decision, she said, "Today starts a new chapter for Black residents of Lowndes County, Alabama, who have endured health dangers, indignities, and

racial injustice for far too long.": "Departments of Justice and Health and Human Services Announce Interim Resolution Agreement in Environmental Justice Investigation of Alabama Department of Public Health." U.S. Department of Justice Office of Public Affairs, May 4, 2023. U.S. Department of Justice (DOJ). https://www.justice.gov/opa /pr/departments-justice-and-health-and-human-services-announce -interim-resolution-agreement.

184. we worked with the National Resources Defense Council and the Southern Poverty Law Center, to persuade the EPA's Office of Environmental Justice and External Civil Rights to open a broad investigation of the Clean Water State Revolving Fund: "EPA Launches Civil Rights Investigation into Alabama Department of Environmental Management Over Sanitation Inequity in Black Communities." NRDC, October 4, 2023. Natural Resources Defense Council (NRDC). https://www.nrdc .org/press-releases/epa-launches-civil-rights-investigation-alabama -department-environmental-management.

10. I AM THE ANSWER TO MY ANCESTORS' PRAYERS

189. the terrible statistics about the killing of Black women: that they are murdered with more than six times the frequency of their white counterparts: Waller, Bernadine Y., Victoria A. Joseph, and Katherine M. Keyes. "Racial Inequities in Homicide Rates and Homicide Methods among Black and White Women Aged 25–44 Years in the USA, 1999–2020: A Cross-Sectional Time Series Study." *The Lancet* 403, no. 10430 (March 2024): 935–45. https://doi.org/10.1016/s0140-6736(23)02279-1.

190. "Do not be anxious about anything, but in every situation, by prayer and petition, with thanksgiving, present your requests to God. And the peace of God, which transcends all understanding, will guard your hearts and your minds in Christ Jesus": Phil. 4:6–7 (New International Version).

195. Lott Carey, a once-enslaved preacher who managed to buy his freedom from his owners in Virginia in 1813: "Our History." Lott Carey Global Christian Missional Community. Accessed May 29, 2024. https://lottcarey .org/about/.

196. what Jesus urged in Matthew 25:40, "Whatever you did for one of the least of these brothers and sisters of mine, you did for me": Matt. 25:40 (New International Version).

198. two days after the horrific mass shooting in Emanuel Church, families of victims appeared to face Dylann Roof: Berman, Mark. "'I Forgive You.' Relatives of Charleston Church Shooting Victims Address Dylann Roof." *Washington Post*, June 19, 2015. https://www.washingtonpost.com /news/post-nation/wp/2015/06/19/i-forgive-you-relatives-of-charleston -church-victims-address-dylann-roof/.

199. In the spring of 2023, in Nashville, Tennessee, three nine-year-old children and three adults at the Covenant School, were murdered by a twenty-eight-year-old gunman, armed with an AR-15: Andone, Dakin. "Nashville School Shooter Fired 152 Rounds during the Attack, Which Was Planned 'Over a Period of Months,' Police Say." CNN, April 3, 2023. https://www.cnn.com/2023/04/03/us/covenant-school-shooting-nashville -tennessee-monday/index.html.

199. three days later thousands of demonstrators appeared at the state-house in Nashville: Jones, Vivian, and Melissa Brown. "Tennessee Capitol Protest Explainer: Here's What Did and Did Not Happen." *The Tennessean*, April 4, 2023. https://www.tennessean.com/story/news /politics/2023/04/04/tennessee-capitol-protest-heres-what-did-and-did -not-happen/70075823007/.

199. In 2021, Tennessee lawmakers passed a measure making permits optional for handguns and weeks before the shooting, some GOP representatives were championing legislation to expand permit-less open carry laws to include long guns: Davis, Chris. "Tenn. Republicans Propose Bills That Would Get the State Closer to 'True' Constitutional Carry for Firearms." News Channel 5 Nashville (WTVF), February 13, 2023. https://www.news channel5.com/news/tenn-republicans-propose-bills-that-would-get-the -state-closer-to-true-constitutional-carry-for-firearms.

199. Among the demonstrators were two young Black lawmakers, Representatives Justin Jones and Justin Pearson . . . and a white woman, Representative Gloria Johnson: McGrady, Clyde, and Emily Cochrane. "'The Justins' Follow a Legacy of Resistance in Tennessee." *New York Times*, April 14, 2023. https://www.nytimes.com/2023/04/14/us /justin-pearson-justin-jones-tennessee.html.

199. House Speaker Cameron Sexton vowed that the representatives would face "consequences": Loller, Travis, Gary Fields, and Adrian Sainz. "Tennessee Becomes New Front in Battle for American Democracy."

AP News, April 8, 2023. https://apnews.com/article/tennessee-expulsion
-democracy-election-nashville-c1ea281cce30e62cb392fca1df30ad3a.

200. Another representative who sponsored the resolution to expel them described their protests against gun violence, their outrage at more senseless
slaughter, as a mere "temper tantrum": Ibid. 9.

200. "Is what's happening outside these doors by Tennesseans who want to
see change a 'temper tantrum'?": Coghill, Arianna. "Justin Pearson,
Tennessee Democrat Expelled for Gun Control Protest, Is Reinstated."
Mother Jones, April 12, 2023. https://www.motherjones.com/politics/2023/04
/justin-pearson-tennessee-democrat-expelled-for-gun-control-protest-is
-reinstated/.

201. A Pew study revealed that 41 percent of white evangelicals own a gun,
compared with 30 percent of others in the US: Shellnutt, Kate. "Packing
in the Pews: The Connection between God and Guns." *Christianity Today*,
November 8, 2017. https://www.christianitytoday.com/news/2017/november
/god-gun-control-white-evangelicals-texas-church-shooting.html.

202. Governor George Wallace, who famously cried during his 1963 inaugural address, "Segregation now. Segregation tomorrow. And segregation forever": Radio Diaries. "'Segregation Forever': A Fiery Pledge
Forgiven, but Not Forgotten." NPR, January 10, 2013. https://www.npr
.org/2013/01/14/169080969/segregation-forever-a-fiery-pledge-forgiven
-but-not-forgotten.

202. In 1995 . . . He met about two hundred civil rights marchers at the St. Jude
Educational Institute in Montgomery: Bragg, Rick. "Emotional March
Gains a Repentant Wallace." *New York Times*, March 11, 1995. https://www
.nytimes.com/1995/03/11/us/emotional-march-gains-a-repentant-wallace
.html.

Acknowledgments

Implicit in the final essay in this collection, "I Am the Answer to My Ancestors' Prayers," is a powerful feeling of gratitude. Gratitude for my parents and my daughter, my grandchildren and my siblings. Gratitude for the vast community of people, including my mosaic of cousins, who appeared in my life at crucial points of my journey and lifted me up. Gratitude for my faith and for the sustaining power of God, who continues to work in mysterious ways in my life.

There is a special joy in being able to complete this book with very specific expressions of gratitude to so many people whose inspiration and sheer hard work led to its publication. First of all, I must thank my friend Nancy Hendrix who has been an angel, connecting me to many people who have been significant in my growth. We met at EJI and have been joined at the hip ever since. Lawanna Kimbro, the master inspirer, for your notes of encouragement, I thank you. Bryan Stevenson, I am deeply grateful that you gave me the space to thrive and believed in me when others did not. My profound gratitude to Laurene Powell Jobs, for being who you are. The world has yet to learn the extent to which you have made it a better place for so many.

The team at Spiegel & Grau has given me a special home, sustaining me during moments of doubt and leading me to this singular accomplishment. I remember my first meeting with Julie Grau, whom I knew as the publisher of Bryan Stevenson's *Just Mercy*. She believed that my stories needed to be read by many. I trusted her, and from that friendship blossomed this book. Thank you, Julie. Andrew Tan-Delli Cicchi has brought his brilliance to all aspects of this endeavor, from his careful reading of early drafts and pitch-perfect editorial suggestions to his diligent work of managing the citations, organizing the proofs, and keeping us all in the loop. Andy and I share a Duke affiliation, but he is clearly one of their graduates who does the institution proud.

Marianne Szegedy-Maszak and I have collaborated in producing this book, and I know how much I will miss our time together, poring over each paragraph and trying to make it shine. Out of this process grew a lasting friendship.

When I first met Mel Berger at William Morris Endeavor, I wasn't sure what to expect from a renowned agent working for a storied agency. What I found was someone warm, empathetic, "a real mensch," and what it means to be "the best in the business." I am so lucky to work with him, the ever-on-top-of-things Cashen Conroy, and his entire team.

The responsibilities of my communications team at FGS Global have grown ever more complicated in recent years, and they have risen to many occasions with efficiency, care, and attention to more details than I can count. A special shout-out to Anne Larimer Hart, Reese Ravner, Federico Araujo, and Deb Greenspan for all that they do. My colleagues at CREEJ have had to work around me as I wrote this book and was a bit distracted at times, but they made sure that our mission continued, and we remain single-minded in our focus. I must offer a special thanks to Lynda Black, my sister from another mother, who takes care of so many aspects of my life that she makes everything possible. A special note of gratitude to my board, especially the magical Jane Fonda and the extraordinary Kat Taylor.

A very special thank-you to former vice president Al Gore, who has moved from being a mentor to a trusted friend. His daughter Karenna Gore also deserves a note of gratitude for bringing spirituality to the work of climate activism.

I have found a second home of sorts at Duke University thanks to my fellow country girl—though from West Virginia, not Alabama—Toddi Steelman, who was there to encourage and guide me. That home was only enhanced by the presence of professors Erika Weinthal, Betsy Albright, and Lori Bennear at the Nicholas School of the Environment who continued to support and encourage me.

But my real center of gravity is with the Huntsville community. Especially my thanks goes to: Cathy Miller, Kenny Anderson, Peggy Steger, Loye Pine, Karen Stanley, Dr. Anne Marie Reidy, Laura Hall, and the HudsonAlpha family. My friends at NASA, Niki Werkheiser, Art Werkheiser, Raymond "Corky" Clinton, and Paul E. Hintze for encouraging and inspiring innovation.

The people at the Aspen Institute have been unfailingly supportive, with special mentions to Greg Gershuny, Beatrijs Kuijpers, Jade Rouse, Catherine Pollack, Kate Jaffee, and Clarke Williams.

General Russel Honoré is the leader of the Green Army and my North Star when I look for guidance related to climate and environmental justice. My other sources of information and inspiration are at NRDC, Earthjustice, RMI, and Climate Reality. A special shout-out to Anna Sewell for untangling the complexities of our case for this book and to her and Neil Gormley for their continued work on the litigation.

And deepest thanks to Dr. Peter Hotez, a "genius" himself who helped me join those ranks. From Karenna and Peter, I have learned that science and religion not only can coexist but are deeply interconnected.

My thanks to everyone who read this manuscript in various stages: my beautiful daughter, Taylor Foster, David Person, Michael Graham, Lynda Black, and Nancy Hendrix.

A special thanks to Mayor Chokwe Lumumba and Danyelle Holmes who so generously shared the triumphs and the struggles of Jackson, Mississippi, with me.

I would not be who I am were it not for my family—Ronald, Gregory, Blanche, Jay C, and David, as well as a host of nieces and nephews—and for the people of Lowndes County, Alabama. They all continue to teach me, inspire me, bring me joy, and remind me I will always have a home there.

And to my partner, James; his son, Justin; daughter, Jordan; and sister, Adrian: You have entered my life as this book came into being and expanded my circle of support through your presence. James, especially, has kept me grounded, made the manuscript more perfect, and reminded me of the possibilities yet to come. Thank you for being there, always.

Finally, my daughter, Taylor, and her wife, Zan, have not only given me two blessed grandchildren but the kind of love and support mothers everywhere dream of from their daughters. This book is as much their legacy as mine.

Huntsville, Alabama
June 2024

About the Author

CATHERINE COLEMAN FLOWERS is an internationally recognized environmental activist and founder of the Center for Rural Enterprise and Environmental Justice (CREEJ). She has dedicated her life's work to advocating for equal access to clean water, air, sanitation, and soil to reduce health and economic disparities in poor and rural communities across the United States. A MacArthur "Genius Grant" recipient, Flowers sits on the board of directors of The Climate Reality Project, the Natural Resources Defense Council, and RMI. She has served as vice chair of the Biden administration's inaugural White House Environmental Justice Advisory Council and is a practitioner-in-residence at the Nicholas School of the Environment at Duke University. She is the author of *Waste: One Woman's Fight Against America's Dirty Secret*, and her essays have appeared in the *New York Review of Books* and the *New York Times*, among other publications. In 2023, Flowers was recognized as one of *TIME*'s 100 Most Influential People in the world and was featured on *Forbes*' 50 Over 50 list.

Learn more at www.catherinecolemanflowers.com.